Praise for Farhana (
Secrets of the Kashmir

G000057529

SPECIAL NEW EDI`..-...`

"A brilliant read. This book reveals why human security is a global issue."
— U.S. Ambassador Prudence Bushnell

"Qazi brings the colors, smells, people and politics of Kashmir to life. The only thing more enlightening would be to travel there yourself."
— Porter Fox, Editor, *Nowhere Magazine*

"Qazi's bravery, open-mindedness, intelligence and tenacity take her into danger, real lives, raw emotions and ultimately discovery. This is a book that must be read by those who wish to deeply understand the motivations, lives and thoughts behind women in Kashmir. This book is unique in its perspective, thoughtfulness and human experiences."
— Robert Young Pelton, Best-selling Author & Filmmaker

"In *Secrets of the Valley*, Qazi skillfully connects us to the intense, complex and remarkably strong women of Kashmir. Their fascinating and emotionally touching stories are deeply moving and need to be heard. Rich with detail, this powerful book provides emotional insight into this divided region."
— Ross Kauffman, Academy Award- winning Filmmaker

"*Secrets of the Kashmir Valley* confirms Qazi as a graceful writer. This is a generous book of the heartache and soul of a people struggling to survive the politics of genocidal war."
— Riaz Khokhar, former Foreign Secretary and Pakistan Ambassador to the United States

"A fascinating look at the women of Kashmir and their struggle for freedom. A must read."

— Souheila Al-Jadda, Peabody Award- winning Producer and Journalist

"Farhana Qazi skillfully weaves the lives and voices of the Muslim women in South Asia into the broader fabric of a region long known for its breath-taking beauty, religious devotion, and heart-stopping violence. With deep empathy but unblinking candor, Qazi portrays Kashmir and its conflict-haunted inhabitants with a dignity and complexity that is often missing in other accounts. Going where others have feared to tread, Qazi leverages her local heritage and Western analytical training in a way that blends historical narrative, travelogue, and reportage into a poignant and colorful portrayal of her own family as well as the lives of women in Kashmir."

— Timothy Hollifield, Lieutenant Colonel, U.S. Army (Retired)

"In writing both sensitive and beautiful, Farhana Qazi examines the lives and choices of women seeking and creating their empowerment in a place that for six decades has been an object of war. This is an important book for women and for us all.

— Diane Thomas, Author of *In Wilderness*

"Farhana Qazi, a Texan of Pakistani descent, has written a shimmering book about her encounters with the women of Kashmir, starting with her own mother, who joined the Pakistani Army in the 1970s to fight for Kashmir. Qazi travelled to this land of haunting beauty to interview activists and advisors, protestors and politicians, mothers and martyrs, educators and entertainers, and more. The result is a moving journey through what has been called "the most beautiful prison in the world."

— Deborah Scroggins, Author of *Wanted Women*

"Qazi's brilliant book combines her unique personal experience with her deep knowledge of the region, its people and its culture to tell us a story far more informative about today's events than any intelligence brief. And it is beautifully written--a joy to read."

— Brian Michael Jenkins, Scholar

"*Secrets of the Valley* is an important book that unveils the quintessential role of women in one of the most contested areas of the world. It is a deeply touching and personal story that pulls us closer to the women and men in Kashmir."

— Seth G. Jones, Director, Transnational Threats Project, The Center for Strategic & International Studies

"Kashmir is too often seen through the prism of the violence in and around it due to its geopolitical situation. Farhana Qazi, whose grandmother is from Kashmir, gives us an extraordinarily different perspective with a focus on women. For anyone who wishes to understand this land of poets and mystics, this is essential reading."

— Akbar Ahmed, Best-selling Author and Ibn Khaldun Chair of Islamic Studies, American University, Washington, DC

"This secrets of Kashmir's moving stories of genocide and persecution are revealed here in this book most beautifully by my friend Farhana, an award-winning speaker who must be heard globally. This book begs the question why again when humanity declared Never Again!"

— Amineh Hoti, Award-winning Author; Founder of the Centre for Knowledge, Dialogue & Action

"A gripping narrative tracing the lives of disparate women set against a common backdrop of conflict. Leveraging the advantage of her sensitivity as an insider yet the objective reflections of an outsider, Farhana weaves an empathetic account chronicling the experiences, choices and responses of these women giving a rare insight into the psychology of women in conflict. It is a refreshing addition to a yet evolving body of literature on women, their role, agency and outlook in the Kashmir conflict."

— Asma Khan Lone, Political Activist and Professor, New Delhi, India

"Qazi gives us insights into rarely visible Kashmir. Her powerful narrative and sensitive, brilliant storytelling, reveal her personal background and in-depth research experiences in Kashmir. A highly skilled writer, Qazi also provides a heart-and-soul connection for the reader that has been featured in organized panels at the United Nations."
— Lois A. Herman, Coordinator of the Women's United Nations Report Network, Switzerland

"From a line of fierce, beautiful women, Ms. Qazi starts with her own mother and grandmother, giving voice to the women of Kashmir, survivors who have fought for their rights and their own self-determination. Her writing, like Farhana herself, is charming, compassionate, compelling, and a must-read for women's studies readers who seek to understand gender roles in conflict, and students interested in South Asia. Those of us who simply enjoy character development will be drawn into Farhana Qazi's tapestry of stories."
— Sherra Babcock, Vice President, Chautauqua Institution, New York

"Inspiring. Qazi writes with compassion as she traces the lives of women in Kashmir."
— Salman Ahmed, Musician, Actor and Author of *Rock And Roll Jihad*

"Farhana Qazi is a one-woman interdisciplinary team. In this remarkable book, through a series of evocative interviews, Qazi takes the reader into the world of Muslim women in the contested terrain of Kashmir. Drawing on her rich cultural background, she leads the readers to understand how these are individual journeys but at the same time reflect collective identity that is bred in the bone."
— Jerrold M. Post, M.D., Author of *The Of The Terrorist*

"*Secrets of the Valley* is a penetrating book written in prose, mixed with politics and intimate family stories, to create a powerful parable for our times that moves and educates the reader on a forgotten place. Qazi not only tells us the heart rending stories of her own family but also had the courage to traverse Kashmir to bring back the voices of women living and suffering there today."

— Anne Speckhard, Director of the International Center for the Study of Violent Extremism; Washington, D.C.

"Qazi's beautifully crafted and sensitively told tale reveals in profound ways the too often untold or elided over story of women in engaged in multifaceted and multilayered struggles in one of the world's least understood regions. She takes you to the heart--literally and figuratively-- of Kashmir, of struggle, and of women's lives...and her own. This powerful book is a compelling reminder of Rukeyser's axiom that the universe is made of stories not atoms."

— Eric Selbin, Ph.D., Author of *Revolution, Rebellion, Resistance*

"Qazi has highlighted key issues on Kashmir that will help readers better understand South Asia's long-standing conflict."

— Abdul Latif, Editor, *Kashmir Watch*

"Filled with nuance and beautifully narrated, *Secrets of the Valley* provides a hauntingly intimate and movingly compassionate portrait of Kashmir. Qazi deftly navigates the complex politics, vexed histories, and difficult terrain of a divided region. Ethnographic and autobiographical, provocative and evocative, heartbreaking and hopeful, *Secrets of the Valley* gives its readers a powerful, dynamic picture of both people and place."

— Cathy J. Schlund-Vials, Author Of *War, Genocide, And Justice*

"Qazi gives meaning and understanding to the Kashmir issue that goes much deeper than the facts and legal arguments. She gives the reader a riveting view of the people most affected by this conflict. Written with raw emotion, pain and hope, Qazi lived this book, risked her life for it, and spent time away from family to tell one of the greatest stories about the women of Kashmir.

— Todd Shea, Founder Of Comprehensive Disaster Relief Services, Pakistan

"Farhana Qazi's vivid detail, personal experience and history of South Asia make this book a gripping read."

— Omer Dossani, Filmmaker

"The forgotten story of the people of Kashmir is brought to the world by an author who most qualified to write on the subject. The story of Kashmiri women is the story of Qazi's home, her childhood, and her extended family."

— Ibrahim Nasar, Voice of America

"A very compelling book written smartly with so much passion and creativity."

— Anjum Malik, Co-Founder, Al- Hambra Chamber of Commerce

"Qazi gives us a useful and pleasant narrative of some unpleasant realities that are frequently being faced in India and Pakistan. Written more like a novel, this book provides new, deep and interesting insights into the 'veil of Kashmir' that are based on personal and authentic observations. The compelling arguments of the book will certainly draw attention to the rulers in New Delhi, Islamabad and the United Nations to the dangers of the unresolved issue of Kashmir."

— Raza Muhammad Khan, Lt Gen, Pakistan Army (Ret)

"Farhana Qazi's narrative on the conflict is a valuable addition to the literature on Kashmir."

— Shabir Choudhry, Director of The Institute of Kashmir, United Kingdom

ALSO BY FARHANA QAZI

Untold Truths of the Kashmir Valley

Kashmir Is Heaven Enough

Invisible Martyrs

SECRETS OF THE KASHMIR VALLEY

SPECIAL NEW EDITION

Farhana Qazi

Newport Publishing

First edition published by Pharos Media (2016)

Library of Congress Cataloging-in-Publication Data
Qazi, Farhana, 2020
Secrets of the Kashmir Valley: a personal journey to one of the world's oldest conflicts – special new edition

Book design and type formatting by Farhana Qazi
Printed in the United States of America
ISBN 979-8-6658314-2-8 pbk
ISBN 978-0-9994102-1-9 ebook

✺ Created with Vellum

To the people of Kashmir

"Those who deny freedom to others, deserve it not for themselves."

--Abraham Lincoln, civil rights activist and the 16th President of the United States

"Truth never damages a cause that is just."

--Mahatma Gandhi, leader of India's independence movement

FOREWORD

Kashmir remains a place of great beauty but also of tragedy. In my own travels in the region, both literal and figurative, I have found pain and yet joy. The pain I attribute to a longing for peace, combined with the anguish of people who do not feel that they are masters of their own destiny; the joy I see because of the sheer magnificence of the location and the pride of being 'from Kashmir'. Thousands of people of Kashmiri origin are of course now scattered throughout the world, in Britain, Europe, and the United States. Some are political exiles, some left voluntarily simply for what they believed was a better life. But the longing to remain connected with their homeland remains.

Farhana Qazi's book *Secrets of the Valley* is testimony to one individual's feeling for Kashmir, although her home is in Texas. The subtitle – *A Personal Journey to the War in Kashmir between India and Pakistan* – reveals the harsh realities of a region which – ever since India and Pakistan became independent countries in 1947 – has been the subject of rival claims. Three wars have been fought with the former Princely state of Jammu and Kashmir serving as the *casus belli*: in 1947-1949 and briefly in 1965 and 1999.

Yet still the issue is unresolved: the promised plebiscite has never been held; endless peace talks have failed. The state remains *de facto* divided on the ground. Two-thirds is under Indian administration – which includes the beautiful Valley of Kashmir, the sparsely inhabited yet magnificent region of Ladakh and Jammu. One-third is administered by Pakistan: this region includes the narrow strip of land watered by the Jhelum river which leads tantalizing onwards to the Valley and what was formerly called the 'Northern Areas' now Gilgit-Baltistan, whose lofty peaks rise to join those of the Himalayas.

Divided along a ceasefire line – known as the 'line of control' - there is no formally recognized international frontier and so the state is classified as 'disputed territory'. As Farhana Qazi points out, the state's history has created several anomalies one of which is that it now has three capitals – two in Indian-administered Jammu and Kashmir – Srinagar, the summer capital, Jammu, the winter capital; and Muzaffarabad, the capital of Pakistan-administered Kashmir.

Another incongruity is the different names used by Indians and Pakistanis to describe the areas they administer. While Indians refer to the state under their control simply as Jammu and Kashmir, Pakistanis call it Indian-Held Kashmir (IHK); and while the Pakistanis refer to the area the Pakistani government administers as Azad (Free) Jammu and Kashmir (AJK) - sometimes Azad Kashmir for short - Indians refer to it as Pakistani-Occupied Kashmir (POK). This stems from the belief in India that, by virtue of Maharajah Hari's Singh's 1947 Instrument of Accession, the whole state legally is part of India, and from the belief in Pakistan that the Indian government is 'holding' onto the state against the wishes of the inhabitants

Part history, part memoir, through her own travels, bravely venturing from the comfort of her Texas home, Qazi shares with the reader some of the stories of those she encounters, revealing a land where contradictions are manifest – Kashmir, a land of conflict; and Kashmir, a haven where people wish to travel to experience its manifold beauty.

As a woman, her focus has been creating 'an oral history of women and their men.' And for Qazi, the first oral history is that of her mother, who unusually joined the Pakistani Army in 1959 to fight for Kashmir, a land she had held onto 'like a timeless picture in a vintage frame' believing, as did many of the older generation of Pakistanis, that because its population was predominantly Muslim, it should have become part of Pakistan when the subcontinent was partitioned. Subsequent chapters focus on the lives of those who have taken up the struggle – 'Martyrs', 'Prisoners', 'Wives of Militants' and 'Refugees'.

The narrative is both moving and compelling: we encounter Sadia the 'bomb girl', who chose to do more than 'stay at home or protest'; Anjum, fighting to free prisoners; Samie, a potential politician; Asiya, the well-known militant activist—all of whose individual oral histories make up a collective chronicle of suffering and struggle.

Whenever I speak or write about the troubled situation in the Valley of Kashmir, I, too, am optimistic—my belief founded on the strong individuals I, like Farhana Qazi have met, whose endurance is extraordinary. I like to envisage that there will be a resolution of the conflict, so that the characters so movingly portrayed in this book, and many others like them, can enjoy the beauty and tranquility of their land, living peacefully and with dignity into old age.

Victoria Schofield, author of *Kashmir in the Crossfire* and *Kashmir in Conflict*

AUTHOR'S NOTE

Kashmir is an active conflict. It is unsettling and unpredictable. Every day, someone dies. Someone is detained. Or someone disappears. The valley of death is also described as 'Paradise on Earth.' But in this land of magic and myth, there are madmen and militaries that trample on Kashmir's beauty. After six decades of war, Kashmiris go on living. They go to school. They fall in love. They get married. Many have children. They do what seems normal, despite the protests, politics, and paranoia of living in a place that is not free.

My first visit to Kashmir helped me see the conflict through the eyes of women and their men. Return visits and constant contact with local Kashmiris made me aware of torture, trauma and terrible life-altering incidents. I entered the private world of women. They welcomed me and engaged me, as I had come from America to see them and listen to their stories. The brief periods I spent in Kashmir tormented me for years to come. I never thought I would fall hopelessly in love with a land of torrential beauty, and a people softened by the traumas of conflict.

Meeting with the women of Kashmir has been risky and rewarding. In this book, I describe encounters with mothers of martyrs, wives of militants, prisoners, protestors, and political activists. The women interviewed have one thing in common. They want a separate country called Kashmir. They demand self-determination. They fight for freedom.

It is because of their struggle and sacrifices that I have chosen to conceal their true names, when necessary. I have a duty to protect them because they gifted me with history through their eyes. Each woman has a story to share. As a collection, these stories are a source of Kashmir's modern struggle. The women of Kashmir have shown me compassion and courage. And so I write, because I dance between both cultures and have a moral duty to share their triumph and trauma. My unspoken promise to Kashmir is that I will hold its closely guarded secrets. I will forever keep that promise.

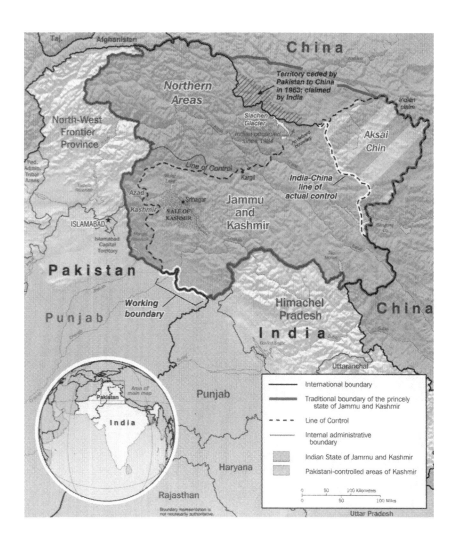

Taj.   Afghanistan

C h i n a

Northern
Areas

Territory ceded by
Pakistan to China
in 1963; claimed
by India

Indian
claim

North-West
Frontier
Province

Siachen
Glacier
Indian occupied
since 1984

Aksai
Chin

Fed.
Admin.
Tribal
Areas

Line of Control

Kargil

India-China
line of
actual control

Azad

Srinagar

Jammu
and
Kashmir

Kashmir

VALE OF
KASHMIR

ISLAMABAD

Islamabad
Capital
Territory

P a k i s t a n

Working
boundary

Himachel
Pradesh

C h i n a

P u n j a b

I n d i a

Uttaranchal

Area of
main map

Pakistan

Punjab

India

Haryana

Rajasthan

Boundary representation is
not necessarily authoritative.

Uttar Pradesh

————	International boundary
————	Traditional boundary of the princely state of Jammu and Kashmir
- - - -	Line of Control
··········	Internal administrative boundary
▨	Indian State of Jammu and Kashmir
▨	Pakistani-controlled areas of Kashmir

0   50   100 Kilometers
0   50   100 Miles

INTRODUCTION
WELCOME TO WONDERLAND

"It would be difficult to describe the colors, which are seen on the
Kashmir mountains."
--SIR WALTER LAWRENCE, 1895

"Here, we have the most splendid amphitheater in the world."
–AN AMERICAN TRAVELER, 1914

This book was started when I was a child. When Mama first said the word "Kashmir," I thought she imagined it, like a fairytale with wondrous characters imbued with magic. In books, Kashmir is described as the land with a floating vegetable garden, a palace named after fairies called *Pari Mahal*, hundreds of houseboats made of the fragrant deodar tree along Dal Lake, and gardens with majestic fountains built by India's long-gone royal emperors. Later, I realized Mama didn't imagine Kashmir. It was real.

Growing up in Texas, in the capital city of Austin, I never heard of Kashmir in school or saw it on the map. I didn't know the word Kashmir came from an Indian text. 'Ka' means water and 'shimir' is 'desiccated water.' Together, these phrases reflect Kashmir as 'a land desiccated by water.' Some scholars trace the language of Kashmir, called Kashmiri, to the linguistic roots of Sanskrit—an ancient Indian tongue.

In Kashmir, some speak Urdu, Pakistan's national language. Most understand Hindi, the national tongue of India. In school, Kashmiri children are taught English, a token of British colonialism. These facts were missing from the classroom in Texas, where I went to school.

Kashmir is a tiny valley with nearly 86,000 square miles. A microscopic fraction of the world's population lives in Kashmir. Over ten million people in Jammu and Kashmir reside in the state of India, which is two million more than the population of Virginia, where I now live. Nearly six million Kashmiris live in the autonomous territory of Pakistan.

By contrast, my childhood home in the state of Texas is twice the size of all of Kashmir. The Chinese regions of Aksai Chin and Trans-Karakoram account for 19 percent of Kashmir, a fact disputed by India. At its highest peak is the Siachen Glacier, where Indian and Pakistani troops engage in border clashes like schoolyard bullies. It is the world's highest battlefield, fought at an altitude of 20,000 feet. Only India and Pakistan have waged war over Kashmir. In this vicious cycle, Pakistan loses, India wins, and the Kashmiri people are marginalized all over again.

Over time, I learned that Kashmir is a religious place. Over 60 percent of Kashmiris are Muslims. Other religious groups include Buddhists, Christians, Hindus, Jains, and Sikhs. Buddhism prevailed in Kashmir's old capital, Shrinagari, founded by the Buddhist emperor Ashoka. Hinduism emerged in the 9th century and Islam flourished in the 14th century. Here, religion is deeply embedded in local customs and cultural traditions, reflected in rituals of childbirth, marriage, and death. Given the diverse religious landscape, most Kashmiris are decidedly tolerant.

As long as I can remember, Mama sensationalized Kashmir with war stories. "Kashmir is worth fighting for," she said, trumpeting nationalism. She wanted to prove to herself that she could do something more for Pakistan other than study. "I know men eventually need women to help them. They cannot fight wars alone," she said.

Mama boasted of being a "pure" Kashmiri. At first glance, Kashmiris look distinctly European and have been compared to the Indo-Aryan race. They have unforgettable features, their faces sharpened by sensual eyes, clear skin, and glorious hair. Some Kashmiris could pass for Sicilians.

In those early years, I didn't know what Kashmir had to do with my parents' country of origin, Pakistan. Were Kashmir and Pakistan related? What was special about Kashmir? And why do Kashmiris refer to themselves as a forgotten people? *Who* has made them invisible? Before I had ever visited Kashmir, I began to compare Kashmiris to the Native American Indian tribes—both were people displaced and disgraced by colonial rulers.

Like my parents, I was born in Pakistan. My mother and I share the same birthplace of Lahore, the second largest city and cultural center of Pakistan. My father was born in the industrial city of Gujranwala, also named the 'city of wrestlers' for being the birthplace of South Asia's finest bodybuilders. Situated on the Grand Trunk Road, Gujranwala is connected to my mother's city in the northern Punjab province. While my mother lived in one city, my father moved around the Indian Subcontinent.

When he was younger, his father, a Sergeant in the British Army, was assigned to Agra, Uttar Pradesh—known to the world for the Taj Mahal, built by Mughal emperor Shah Jahan in memory of his wife. They returned to Gujranwala when India and Pakistan gained their independence in August 1947; the countries' national holidays are separated by just one day. Pakistan celebrates its national day on August 14; India observes this on August 15.

No matter how often I visit, Lahore is a place to which I do not inherently belong. I have never lived there. I can only identify with its cuisine, which Mama brought to America when she first arrived in Tennessee in 1970, and then moved to Texas with my father, carrying me in her arms. Mama mastered Lahore's culinary gifts—our house was always infused with *garam masala*, onions, and cardamom.

Most of Lahore is foreign to me. I remember it as a labyrinth of dust-tormented streets and dry, trembling air. It is a city described by English writer Rudyard Kipling as "the growling, flaring, creed-drunk city," noisy and rambunctious like a beating heart. My father reminded me of an old Punjabi saying: *If you have not been to Lahore, you have yet to be born.* The wife of Emperor Jehangir once said of Lahore, "By giving my life for Lahore, I have purchased another Paradise." Once known as the walled city of Lahore, my birthplace prides itself with distinguished Mughal architecture and colonial buildings built by the British.

Access to the walled city is permitted through six of the remaining thirteen gates. One is called the Kashmiri gate because it was built in the direction of Kashmir. Constructed by the Mughals, the gates are landmarks of foreign rule. In 1849, when the British arrived, the walled city was annexed. Having been raised in America, Lahore became a distant memory. As an adult, when I traveled to Indian-held Kashmir, I boarded a plane in Lahore, a short ride to New Delhi, India's capital and my gateway to Paradise.

I had heard enough about Kashmir from Mama and her mother in Pakistan to know it is a deeply divided land. At the heart of Kashmir are its people, trapped in *Wonderland* (between two South Asian rivals, India and Pakistan, who lay claim to all of Kashmir). In this heavily guarded valley, protestors and political activists have so far failed to achieve their goal of an independent Kashmir. Because of the war, life in Kashmir is an assemblage of unknown and unpredictable events. "This is the most beautiful prison in the world," a senior militant told me.

This book is an oral history of Muslim women and their men. It is a series of stories by ordinary Kashmiris living extraordinary lives in an active conflict. It is an attempt to make these invisible women and their men known to the outside world. The story of Kashmir is a matrix of stories of women *inside* the conflict—each with a different version based on individual experiences. That war is a continuum with multiple histories means that women's experiences are bound to change during the various stages of armed conflict. This book brings women's lives to the center of the conflict, putting the spotlight on them as capable, competent, and intelligent actors who deserve greater decision-making power.

Prior to this book, I have given lectures on Muslim Kashmiri women. They are activists and advisors; protestors and politicians; mothers and martyrs; educators and entertainers, and much more. When I think of the women of Kashmir, I am reminded of W.H. Auden, who said, "All I have is a voice."

This book is a tribute to the multitude of Muslim voices rising in Kashmir to oppose a conflict that has lasted over seventy years. These women are the victims of war. On March 8, 2013, celebrated as International Women's Day, I presented a slideshow at the United Nations in New York to explain reasons why Kashmiri women protest.

Prestige. Women are as capable as men. Women protest to preserve their honor, acknowledging that their progress depends on their participation.

Power. Women are persuasive speakers and political party leaders. Even stay-at-home mothers take to the streets because they know they can save their families when they collectively call for change.

Protect. Women nourish their children and men. They will do anything to shield their families from harm and defend against human rights violations.

Peace. Women want to end the conflict by being a voice in the non-violent movement for independence. They are determined to break the cycle of abuse. They lead political parties and movements as protectorates of marginalized populations within their society.

More recently, I have been teaching Gender, Security and Conflict at my alma mater, The George Washington University in Washington, D.C., America's capital city. Inside the classroom, I introduce students to concepts of gender theory with a focus on how it is applied to understanding issues of security and the dynamics of armed conflict, peacekeeping and peace building. The course includes a section on gender-based violence in armed conflict and we examine the women of Kashmir—this book also examines the horrific crimes of rape, and the lack of gender-just reparations for the victims. Gender-based violence is a predominant feature of many armed conflicts internationally, and it is no secret that across the valley women are constantly patronized all the time by the military, militants, and other men.

Despite these abuses, women rise up. The unfolding story of Kashmir must include the different stories of Muslim women; many have redefined their roles in the conflict. To begin, the book explores the story of Kashmir beginning in my childhood home in Texas and my birthplace of Pakistan, followed by the militarized zone in India-held Kashmir, where my grandmother once lived. This is a personal narrative, though it is only one part of the larger story. The focus of this book is the war histories told by women.

This book reveals the multiple ways women experience war and explores their visibility and different ways they meet and mobilize. It includes their aspiration for political power; and their need and desire to be employed and educated. Ultimately, women will do what it takes to be empowered. All across Kashmir, women deserve human security—the right to political, social, economic, health, and food needs. Human security is an all-encompassing concept I learned from U.S. Ambassador Prudence Bushnell, my mentor and friend. With access to human security, a people can enjoy peaceful living.

Like their men, women in Kashmir feel a sense of urgency to resolve the conflict. These women are determined, dedicated, and destined for change. They are the main survivors of war. With entry into their homes, offices, and prisons, this book is a chronicle of Kashmir's personal stories shared by its women. This book highlights select stories of female survivors—political activists fighting for gender rights; the mothers of martyrs; female prisoners falsely accused of terrorism; and more. The stories are painstakingly real and divulge the shocking secrets that permeate the lives of Kashmiri women.

The women (and men) interviewed, and the places visited for this book cover a decade of research. As of this writing, I maintain daily contact with Kashmiris to continuously document the untold truths that are prevented by censorship, communication blackouts, lock-downs, curfews, and the ongoing COVID-19 pandemic. In this volatile environment, as people and events are likely to change, so do the people of conflict. The excessive use of force and an iniquitous legal system is the norm. It is therefore expected that women alive today may be dead tomorrow.

Finally, in a patriarchal society like Kashmir, men are the first fighters and primary protectorate of women. I have included conversations with men because they often influence, incite or invite women into their political parties and the protest movement. Often, women join the separatist movement because of their men. Hence, this book is not about the particulars of war. Rather, it is about the *people of conflict*.

The story begins with my mother, one of Kashmir's fighters.

Part One

The Story of Kashmir

1

MAMA'S WAR

"Kashmir is worth fighting for."
—NARGIS PERVEEN

"No nation can rise to the height of glory without its women."
--MUHAMMED ALI JINNAH, FOUNDER OF PAKISTAN

Nargis Perveen held the British-made rifle in her small hands. She loaded the Lee-Enfield firearm called the .303 with a five-round charger. She had never held a weapon before. She pressed her thumb against the smokeless powder cartridge and waited for the order to fire. Used by the British military in World War I, the rifle was nearly 45 inches long and weighed between eight to nine pounds. Mama preferred a smaller weapon. She was barely five feet tall and weighed ninety pounds.

In her family, she was the middle child. Her name, Nargis, is the yellow and white daffodil flower grown in India and Pakistan—a flower I remember sprouting like weeds along the highways of Texas in early spring.

I could see Mama clasp her weapon. She had a strong grip. "These are working hands," she often said, opening her weathered palms to prove she could do almost anything. In later years, when she migrated to America, she cut down a dead pecan tree, put up a fence, and once, I watched her slice the throat of a chicken with a large knife on the porch.

In her youth, Mama looked like a Geisha, with pale skin and thin lips. Mama has Aryan-like features. Her eyes match her hair. She has high-cheek bones and a flawless complexion. She was a beauty like my grandmother, Imtiaz Mir, whom I affectionately called Nano.

Mama adjusted her uniform. She sported a pair of straight khaki pants with a long *kameez* (shirt), the color of a sparrow that covered her hips. She let her hazelnut-colored hair hang loose on her shoulders. The Pakistani Army adored her. They called her the "jewel of the East."

"The Army used to look at my rosy cheeks and said I had good blood! They insisted I donate my blood to dying soldiers in the war," she said with a bout of laughter. "But I never did. I thought it was better to join the war. By joining the Army, I had to prove to my country that women are equal to men. That I can fight."

In faded black and white photographs, I see a striking resemblance between Mama and Habba Khatoon, a 16th century Muslim mystic poetess from Kashmir, whose songs still vibrate throughout the valley. But unlike Khatoon, who created some of the most beautiful poetry and songs as she wandered the valley in search for love, Mama used her voice to assert herself as a young woman in a patriarchal and patrilineal country. And while Khatoon was affectionately called *Zoon*, a Kashmiri word for moon, Mama's nickname is *Mito*, an Urdu word for parrot. That explains why she always has something to say.

Mama was high-spirited, high-strung and highly emotional. At the age of fourteen, when Mama finished the equivalence of high school, she joined a government college in Lahore. At the time, many Pakistanis like Mama were tired of one military failure after another. "People needed change. Each military ruler failed us," she said. This was the 1960s. Pakistan was on the verge of another war with India, and it needed women to fight alongside its men.

Commander Malik was in charge of the young women. They gathered in the Lahore stadium, a cricket ground built in 1959. In later years, the stadium was renamed Gaddafi Stadium after the late Libyan tyrant, Colonel Muammar al-Gaddafi. Mama was among the first recruits. She was a volunteer, the only student in a college of two hundred women who joined the Pakistani Army. I do not think of my mother as a warrior. Even though she can be fierce and fiery, she is a no-nonsense and matter-of-fact woman. Bold and blunt, Mama hurls her opinion like darts, a warrior without fear.

Military men did not expect women to fight. As an adult, when I trained U.S. servicemen and women, I met women who confirmed what Mama knew to be true in Pakistan: an age-old story of resilient women. A female Lieutenant Colonel, who identified herself by her first name Jennifer, told me, "One of the things that pushed me to join is that women are not compelled to succeed in the U.S. military. When someone tells you can't do something, you do it."

Promoted to Colonel in the summer of 2012, Jennifer doesn't announce her new status "because it has no value [among her peers] but is an important rank" for her. I imagine Mama had similar aspirations for herself, although she also knew it was unusual for women to serve alongside mostly Muslim men in the Pakistani Army. Still, as a young woman, she had already accomplished more than most and proved she was willing to die for Kashmir.

But as Pakistan became desperate and despondent, the Army began seeking female recruits. My mother simply volunteered. Pakistan needed women to help them win the war. Mama learned how to perform basic medical training to heal wounded soldiers. She was taught how and when to shoot a weapon and other civil defense skills. She was given all the tools to make her a fighter and a nationalist.

To die while fighting for Kashmir was considered honorable and heroic, worthy of being called a "martyr." I doubt Mama imagined herself a martyr though she shared women's ambition to do something for Pakistan. With a group of women, Mama embraced the national fervor that gripped the new country as it attempted to reclaim Kashmir during the 1965 war—the second time India and Pakistan collided.

The first war between India and Pakistan over the disputed territory took place months after independence. Pakistan had no chance of winning against India which took most of the ammunition stores and ordnance factories when it became a new nation. In the division of British India, Pakistan received a regular army that numbered no more than 150,000 men.

Since the late 1940s, Pakistan's founder Muhammad Ali Jinnah roused Muslim sentiment for Kashmir. Rallying cries for *Azad Kashmir* (Free Kashmir) helped the septuagenarian gain new recruits to the National Guards in the southern port city of Karachi. Women joined the women's wing of the Guard and participated in self-defense exercises.

One of my former students, originally from Karachi, gifted me an original LIFE magazine from 1948 with a picture of Zeenat Haroon, a member of the Women's National Guard, swinging the bamboo *lathi* (used in stick and cane fighting). Today, the *lathi* is a common weapon used to disperse protestors in Indian-held Kashmir.

With a skeleton Army, Jinnah propped up a rebel force known as *lashkars*, Pashtun tribesmen who lived along the Afghanistan and Pakistan border, to wage Pakistan's first war in Kashmir. India defeated Pakistan. In early 1948, months before Jinnah died in a vehicle while waiting for an ambulance to arrive in Lahore, the United Nations intervened. An agreement was made.

The two rivals agreed to a plebiscite—the people of Kashmir would vote. Interviews with Kashmiri activists suggest that the people would likely have voted to become a separate state. More than seventy years later, Kashmiris haven't been allowed to decide their political future. During the war, Pakistan's famed singer Noor Jahan sang the country's first war song. *Meriya dhool sipahiya tenoo Rab diyan rakhan, aye watan ke sajeelay jawanon mere naghmay tumahre liye hain.* (Oh my love, my God be your protector. Oh you the brave, handsome soldiers of my country, my songs are dedicated to you.)

Mama shared the Army's will to claim a land she had never visited. Her national identity as a Pakistani was linked intricately to Kashmir, a valley off-the-beaten-path that my mother learned from her mother's childhood stories. "I am from Kashmir," she said, but shied away from saying *I am a Kashmiri*. Mama held onto Kashmir like a timeless picture in a vintage frame.

She had romanticized the valley. It is *Janaat* or Paradise, a term coined by the late Mughal emperor Jehangir. In his couplet, he wrote *if there is paradise on earth, it is here, it is here, it is here in Kashmir*. For Mama, the valley had old-world charm. She saw it through iconic photographs, sun-kissed images of a *shikara* gliding along Dal Lake, scenes of mountains cast in blue-green cold, and worshippers at sacred places bobbing their heads like sparrows.

From Mama's hometown in Lahore, Pakistan-held Kashmir is at least a six-hour car ride—a drive she's never taken.

Mama trained for the Army in August when the heat, flies and mosquitos seized the city of Lahore. The days were unbearably humid. With an overarching sky, clouds formed a blanket like dusty cotton. Mama felt the weight of her rifle. She thought it was like any weapon. All she had to do was pull the trigger and shoot.

"Fire!" Commander Malik shouted. "Keep your eye on the target! You're your gun!" A raucous sound filled the stadium and startled the pigeons in the cloudless sky. Mama thought her leader was unpleasant to look at. Malik had the look of a wounded bear with a boyish face, sleepy eyes overcast by bushy eyebrows, a Roman nose, and sun-weathered skin. Typical Punjabi men are known for their masculinity, exhibiting signs of aggression, militancy and boorishness. The other women said he looked like a Pashtun from the Federally Administered Tribal Areas, or the FATA. Mama called it "no-man's-land."

Mama fired. She jolted and lurched backward. The external spring of the .303 surprised her. "I never got used to cycling the bolt. Each time I let go of the trigger, I felt I could hit someone," she told me. Mama pointed at the target that was a hundred yards away. She leaned on the dry grass, her *kameez* stained with dust. The firing of the rifle made a concerto of noises. Her heart pounded. The firing was an endless torrent, worse than a cacophony of birds ascending into the August sky.

Mama said she closed her eyes and chanted a Sufi prayer. *Be constantly occupied instead with listening to God.* Mama was unafraid but justifiably nervous. With twenty other volunteers, she was almost in battle.

As she remembered the war, Mama shuddered. "It was my best kept secret," she said. Mama lied to her mother. After class, she changed into her military uniform in the ladies bathroom. She kept it hidden in her school bag.

"Nano didn't check my bag because she was never home. She left early in the morning to teach and then tutored children after school. She was late every night," she recalled.

On the bus to Qaddafi Stadium, a seven-mile journey from her college, other passengers teased Mama. "Look! Here's Fatima Jinnah!" they laughed at her in uniform, although Mama felt honored to be named after a woman coined the Mother of the Nation. Fatimah Jinnah was one of the leading women of Pakistan and a prominent politician.

Before the birth of Pakistan, she Fatimah closed her dental practice to live with her brother, Muhammad Ali Jinnah, after his wife's death. She stood by her brother on the political campaign trail and helped him raise his only daughter. Years before Benazir Bhutto would enter the political limelight, Fatimah became a role model for women like my mother. Fatimah made it possible for hundreds of Pakistani women to participate in general elections and protest in the civil disobedience movement of the late 1940s.

Mama lived by Muhammad Jinnah's vision for a secular Muslim country where women and minorities were recognized as equal to men. Jinnah was a unique political statesman. In his autobiography of Jinnah, historian Stanley Wolpert wrote: "Few individuals significantly alter the course of history. Fewer still modify the map of the world. Hardly anyone can be credited with creating a nation-state. Muhammad Ali Jinnah did all three."[1] When Jinnah died, Fatimah continued her political activism and stood against Pakistan's military dictator, Ayub Khan, in an unfair contest. Had the election been fair, she would have won.

Knowing my mother, her greatest hero for women's rights was the founder, himself. Before Pakistan was born, Jinnah made numerous speeches to address women's issues, which helped him gain female support for a new Pakistan. To improve the lives of women, Jinnah had to appeal to the country's men. In March 1940, Jinnah addressed a crowd in the northern Indian city of Aligarh:

> "It is a crime against humanity that our women are shut up within the four walls of the houses as prisoners...let us try to raise the status of our women according to our own Islamic ideas and standards. There is no sanction anywhere for the deplorable conditions in which our women have to live. You should take your women along with you as comrades in every sphere of life."[2]

After training, Mama changed back into the school uniform and headed home. She lived like this for three weeks. No one suspected her. She knew Nano and her eldest brother would never approve. Though she wasn't sure about her father, Sheikh Nazir Ahmed. He died of a heart attack when Mama was four. Nano never remarried. She refused a second marriage and depended only on herself, thus braving societal prejudices against working women. Nano said,

> "When women have no choice, they do all they can to survive. I learned to rely on myself. I could trust myself to do the right thing for my children. I needed help but when help is not there, women have to prove they are capable. I had to make money. I was not going to let any man or woman tell me I could not care for my family, no matter how hard it would be."

Mama inherited Nano's strong will and spirit, but there were some things she never understood about her own mother. "She didn't allow me to participate in debate contests!" Mama complained. "Those were the days when few women were allowed to talk or mix with men. But I didn't care."

Luckily for Mama, a senior uncle stepped forward to convince Nano that there was nothing wrong with women and men in the same room. In each competition, Mama won trophies, but Nano threw them away when she moved to America.

"I was fearless. I didn't care," Mama said. *How did she keep it a secret? I imagined it must have been difficult for Mama to lie every day to her mother.* "I told your Nano I was out with friends," she replied, smiling. Nano ruled like an autocrat. She delegated chores to her children and enforced strict traditions. She cursed her children for disobedience.

Over time, Mama became resentful of her mother, calling her mean-spirited. "She curses her own children. She doesn't know how to forgive." I wondered if Mama understood her mother carried a lifetime of pain. As her grandchild, I sympathized with Nano. She had been wounded by history. Hers was a time when Pakistan was not yet created and women enjoyed few rights. Had Nano lived in a different time and perhaps a different place, she might have been able to be truly independent.

Like Mama, Nano could have done anything but wasn't given the chance. "I wanted more out of life," Mama said. "Your grandmother never understood me. I wanted to be a doctor. She said no. Then I selected nursing. Again, she refused. Finally, I said I could be a lawyer because I knew how to win an argument. Nano only allowed me to get a teaching certificate," Mama said.

We stood together in the kitchen, looking out at blanket-like clouds. Within minutes, clouds would parade across the sky, and rain would beat against the shed Mama had built in the backyard to grow squash, juicy green peppers, and fat tomatoes. I asked Mama what she might have been if she had another chance.

"Who knows?" Mama turned to me with glittering eyes. "I could have been a politician."

One summer day in Texas, Mama met Pakistan's first and only female leader, Benazir Bhutto. I introduced Bhutto to my mother after a lecture the leader gave to my university in Texas. Prior to her speech, Bhutto and I had dinner with a group of undergraduate students. The wide-eyed young women were eager to discuss Bhutto's role as a Muslim woman in an Islamic country. "This is unprecedented," said Dr. Eric Selbin, a professor and my lifelong friend. "It must be amazing to have a Muslim woman in power," he said.

When asked about women in Islam, Bhutto turned to me. "Farhana you answer this one," she said. "Muslim women are progressive," I began. "There are endless examples in Islamic history as well as contemporary Muslim countries of women's contribution to their state and society. Fifteen hundred years ago, during the time of Prophet Muhammad," I paused, preparing the Texan women for what they probably did not know. "Muslim women had the right to vote. They inherited property. They could choose whom to marry. They had a right to a career. They could even initiate a divorce."

"The greatest example of a Muslim woman was Khadija. She was a wealthy widow in her early 40s in pre-Islamic Arabia, which later became the Kingdom of Saudi Arabia. She was an orphan, twice widowed, and a noble and wealthy woman. She used her wealth to feed and clothe the poor and took care of her relatives. She earned two titles, 'The Princess of Quraysh,' which was the most powerful Arab tribe of its time, and the 'Pure One,' in honor of her virtue."

Bhutto smiled as I told the story. The room fell silent. I had no idea what anyone was thinking, but I was confident they hadn't heard this before. I continued. "She ran a lucrative caravan business and employed Muhammad before he became a Prophet. Khadija was impressed by her 25-year-old employee. Muhammad was hard working and held the honorific title of *Al-Amin*, the Truthful One. Khadija knew this was the man she wanted to marry. She sent a marriage proposal to Muhammad through her cousin, a Jew. When he accepted, Khadija was married for a third time. She was about 40 years old."

Bhutto waited patiently for me to complete my next sentence. I felt I had betrayed the students by taking attention away from one of Pakistan's most important and short-lived leaders. "And when God chose him as a messenger, Khadija stood by her husband's side. She is the example of a strong, stable, and serene Muslim woman," I concluded. I had so much more to say. The young women smiled and seemed to understand that Muslim women, like any other faith-based group, were diverse, distinct, and different. Throughout modern history, Muslim women had been famous politicians, writers, musicians, poets, social activists, entrepreneurs, and much more.

On occasion, I am invited by the U.S. military and other government agencies to address the role of Muslim women today, a topic that sparks more debate and discussion. On those teaching days, I try to help others appreciate the historical glory of early Muslim women. The early Muslim women were examples of courage and compassion. As a counter-terrorism expert, I also share stories of why *some* Muslim women and girls join terrorists groups; why they do not represent Islam; and how the global community can help mitigate this rising threat. The women of Kashmir are not violent and thus, they are not included in *that* story, except for the story of 'Bomb Girl,' a local Kashmiri girl who is the rare exception.

When I paused, Bhutto expressed her astonishment at the marriage proposal between Khadija and Muhammad, given their age difference. "I did not know about this marriage pact," Bhutto seemed incredulous.

"Yes," I said with an air of optimism. "There are more women like Khadija. Even you are a great example to many young Muslim and non-Muslim women."

In an adjacent conference room, Mama waited for her turn to meet Benazir. It was like a rite of passage. Mama glowed as she posed next to Benazir for a photograph with great humility and honor. That picture was placed over the fireplace mantle in the drawing room. Anyone who visits my parents' home catches a glimpse of two powerful women. In 2007, when a local gunman assassinated Benazir Bhutto, Mama lost interest in Pakistan.

There was only one thing Mama kept as a reminder of her youthful activism—a rifle near the bed. "It was loaded until your father took out the bullets," she said, with a tone of regret.

2

REMEMBRANCE

"Independence is God's greatest gift to a woman."
--NANO

She kept me awake. In the mornings, cries of the muezzin echoed throughout the three-story house. As Nano lay in bed, she prayed by opening and closing her eyes in slow motion. These days, her prayers were short. She had very little to say to God, except that it was time for her to go. She desired death.

"I don't understand You! O Allah! Why am I still alive?" Nano wailed from her bed in Lahore. She turned to me, her eyes magnified by grief and fear. Almost 100 years old, Nano looked exceedingly tired.

She had a thin head of long gray hair, steel gray eyes with a hint of blue that looked like opals at midnight, and hands that felt like old leather. At night, she slept with dangling gold emerald earrings. As she aged, Nano's face withered and her voice cracked between sentences.

Outside, the maid called for Nano to let her know she had

arrived. Nano limped to the black steel gate, with keys rattling in her hand. I trailed behind Nano as she undid the heavy lock. A woman in cotton with a gaunt face, dark skin, and shiny brown eyes said hello.

"You are late again," Nano frowned at her. "Always late. You have no responsibility. You don't know what time it is?"

She apologized. "I have a sick child at home."

"Oh? Your child is sick again?"

"Yes, *Ama*," she said, referring to Nano as mother as a sign of respect. It was unacceptable for younger women, especially maids, to address the woman of the house other than by a title. Since Nano had been widowed, *Ama* seemed appropriate.

The maid walked behind Nano, barefoot, her feet thick with dust. Even with her head bowed to the floor, blotches like ink left permanent scars over her cheeks. I had heard of women like her, whose skin turned a shiny black after working as children in the coal mines. Maybe she was one of them. *Where did Nano find her?* I wondered.

The maid swung her arms, carelessly, holding onto a brightly colored scarf drawn over her shoulder. She made long, sweeping strokes with her arms as Nano gave her a to-do list.

"Make simple rice with lentils for lunch. Wash the dishes and clean these floors. There's laundry in the basket, too. Don't forget to rinse the clothes before hanging them to dry. First, make me tea with a slice of bread and something for my child, too. We can't have breakfast at noon!"

The maid slipped into the kitchen, nodding.

"If you come late again, then don't come at all! I don't need you anymore," Nano whined, as she crawled back into her bed.

I watched the maid in Nano's kitchen, a small space with a gas stove, a steel counter and sink, and a glass cabinet for a few mugs and old china ware. In the adjacent room, there was a refrigerator and a small dining table with platters of fruit and fresh vegetables on top. Despite its size, Nano's kitchen was filled with the comforting scents of cardamom, cinnamon and cloves—common spices she used in most culinary feasts when she was younger. Now that the maid prepared her meals, the aromas of the kitchen no longer belonged to Nano.

"Come," I said, holding her by the arm as we crawled back into the bedroom. Curtains with silver flowers were drawn over a side window. The room felt cold and dark when the bright ceiling lamp was switched off. The walls had a fresh cream-white paint and a dated calendar held by a rusty nail.

Situated in the old quarter of Krishnager, Nano's house once belonged to a Hindu family before Pakistan was a country. In the late 1940s, the family migrated to India when it became an independent state. Even after the freedom movement, the neighborhood retained its Hindu name—*Krishna* is a revered god in Hinduism.

Though Pakistan became her home, Nano's family was once rooted in Kashmir before the valley and the entire Indian Subcontinent became unevenly split by the Partition Plan, drafted by Britain's Sir Cyril Radcliffe, who had never stepped foot in the region.[1] In five weeks, the Radcliffe Line, or the border formally recognized by England and Indian nationalists, divided millions of Christians, Hindus, Muslims, and Sikhs. When they withdrew, the British royals transferred the power of all its 584 princely states to the newly created countries of India and Pakistan, except Kashmir. Some historians suspect the British didn't know what to do with Kashmir so they left it alone. Fast-forward to the present and Kashmir is a complex crisis. *A place without a post office.*[2]

Pakistan's famed literary genius, Bapsi Sidwa in *Cracking India,* and India's celebrated writer, Khushwant Singh in *Train to Pakistan,* set their novels in the time of the mass migration and wrote in English. In her book, Sidwa compared the work of the Radcliffe Commission, which set in motion the Partition Plan, to a "careless card game." Suddenly, millions of people in South Asia were given new identities, including Sidwa who wrote: "Lahore is dealt to Pakistan, Amritsar to India. Sialkot to Pakistan. Panthankot to India. I am a Pakistani. In a snap. Just like that."[3] (The author now lives in Houston, Texas.)

Described as one aspect of history's "original trauma,"[4] over fourteen million people crossed newly drawn borders in search of a new home—the British failed to anticipate that people in fear of their lives would feel compelled to move.[5] In history's largest mass migration, Hindis and Sikhs fled to India and Muslims to Pakistan, traveling along the Grand Trunk Road and the railway built by the British. Millions died because they were murdered by angry mobs or fell sick along the way. Most people traveled by foot for dozens of miles and days to reach the other side of the border. In her book *The Other Side of Silence*, Indian scholar Urvashi Butalia describes Partition in heart-wrenching detail: Women were victims of "widespread sexual savagery; about 75,000 women are thought to have been abducted and raped by men of religions different than their own.

Thousands of families were divided, homes destroyed, crops left to rot, villages abandoned."[6] Many more were unaccounted for. A Harvard University study claims that at least 3.4 million people were "missing" during Partition.[7] Other questions about the mass migration remain a mystery. *How many people moved? Where did they settle down?* As researchers at Harvard University confirm, "involuntary movements are harder to study because they are almost invariably driven...by extraordinary events such as wars, partition, and ethnic/religious strife."[8]

Luckily, Nano's family survived. Her parents left Indian-held Kashmir and crossed the Himalayan Mountains to migrate to the Punjab Province, in what was then called West Pakistan. The majority of Muslims already lived in East Pakistan, which later became modern-day Bangladesh. Partition disrupted families and lives. The word 'partition' is, as Indian scholar Ritu Menon notes, a *metaphor for irreparable loss.* The largest migration in history still brings tears to my father's eyes.

As a child, I heard all their stories. Mama told me about her great aunt, who disguised herself as a man, sporting a Western-style business suit and a fake beard. "She boarded the train [from India] to Pakistan. Because women were killed, she had to hide herself. That was a horrible time," Mama said. Indian writer Butalia, also from Lahore, recalls her mother's own story of leaving the city, returning twice to bring her younger brothers and sister to India: "My father remembers fleeing Lahore to the sound of guns and crackling fire."[9]

Most of the recorded violence occurred between castes and faith —Hindu against Muslim, for example. But instances of Muslims betraying other Muslims also defined the myth of nation building. My father recounted a story of his paternal grandfather, who worked in the city of Calcutta under British rule. When Pakistan was born, my great-great-grandfather returned to his ancestral home in the northern slopes of Pakistan, to reclaim a house he had spent a lifetime building. He soon discovered another Muslim family, who migrated from India, had claimed his property.

"They didn't give him his furniture. The new residents threw out his old clothes and dishes. In those days, there was nothing he could do," my father lamented. The leaders of the two countries, Muhammad Ali Jinnah of Pakistan and Jawaharlal Nehru of India, recognized the devastating impact of Partition as millions fled for safety. They called for peace, but there was little they could do to control the messy migration.

When I was nine, my father and I quietly watched the Hollywood movie called "Gandhi," starring Ben Kingsley. He intended for me to look at history behind the crevices of recorded events. To see the struggle and sacrifices of millions as single events and to appreciate one man's humanity. He read me poems by Muhammad Iqbal, Pakistan's philosopher-poet, and had a special way of teaching me to look beyond images and words. "The Taj Mahal was built at the cost of hundreds of laborers," he said. Now when I look at pictures of the famous relic, I only see men dying.

Nano's house generated many stories. The story of moving into a space previously owned by Hindus, before India or Pakistan declared their independence. The story of everyone living together, even after marriage, as one big joint family. And the story of grandchildren playing on the flat rooftop of the house while Nano, their caretaker, watched with joy. For decades, the house was the center of Nano's life, complete with history and family fables. As her family structure changed, caused by children and grandchildren living separately, the house she once cherished for its infectious love of people rearranged itself into empty spaces.

On occasion, rooms filled with guests. Every few years, Mama visited Nano from Texas and relatives gathered to hear my mother's laughter and joyful stories of life in America. Like Nano, I preferred the warm seclusion of her bedroom, where a wooden armoire stored her clothes and a few items from a distant past. She has an assemblage of beautiful, useful, and livable things to be worn at any time. She held onto her woolen shawls, pieces of gold jewelry, and a large colored picture of her eldest son, Qaisar, who died of a stroke in his mid-fifties in Houston, Texas.

In the midst of her things, a vague memory came back to me: from my early childhood, riding on my uncle Qaisar's back as he pretended to be a horse, my favorite animal. In those early years, he came to live with my family in a small town outside of Nashville, Tennessee. The only other family member to migrate to America from Pakistan, uncle Qaisar was more like a friend, always singing and saying silly things to make my sister and I laugh hysterically. He died too young.

Nano's youngest son, Talat, left Pakistan for Texas, sponsored by a university in Arkansas to pursue post-doctoral research in botany. Settled with his wife and two children, both of whom are studying medicine, my uncle never looked back. Nano's two daughters lived close by and visited often, although it wasn't enough to comfort Nano. She wanted her sons and maybe Mama, who had no reason to return. "My life is here in Texas with your father," she told me. I knew Mama could never leave a garden blooming with jasmine and pink roses.

Nano clung onto her deceased son's pictures, afraid to lose them. When I asked to see a family album, she said she had no photographs of herself or her husband. No pictures of their wedding day or the birth of her five children. So many events in Nano's life were undocumented because photographs were not taken of her. "We didn't have a camera," she said. "What difference would it have made? Everything exists here," she said, touching her forehead. If photography is empathy—a last testament to the identity of a person, place, or a moment in time—then Nano needed images to capture her life's story. She framed her deceased son on the wall across her bed.

"A mother should never outlive her children," she'd say with immense distress. As she continued to age, she began to outlive her friends, siblings, neighbors and other relatives. Given Nano's growing pains, it was a miracle she was still alive.

When Nano was ninety, she was skin and bones. She had few teeth, her spine curved like a yoga ball, and she covered her feet in cotton. In winter, she sported a sweater vest and a simple shawl in summer.

The maid entered the room with a bowl of porridge with rice-grain-shaped kernels. She learned to cook dishes that would be easy for Nano to chew and swallow. Nano perched over the food with disgust. "This is what happens when you can't eat what you want," she whined. She wanted more sugar, a pinch more salt, and perhaps caffeine.

"Go away!" Nano yelled at the servant girl. "You are useless!"

Nano smiled at me. "Tell your uncle in America to stop sending me a maid. I'm capable. Tell him. I know how to cook rice and soup for myself. I can walk, too. Everyone thinks I'm too weak to do anything!"

Nano forgot the time she fell and nearly broke her hip. Or when she had a high fever and whooping cough. When she couldn't move, one of her two daughters came to look after her.

"Women don't usually live alone in Pakistan," I chimed. *Please come back to America*, I thought.

"I hate it when people try to control me. Eat this. Don't eat that. Take this medicine. Go to bed. Stay in bed. This servant girl will make me crazy!"

"Remember, independence is God's greatest gift to a woman," Nano said, proudly.

Yes, Nano. No one can tell you what to do in your own home. No man or child can control the way you feel, think or act. You are free and alone. If only Nano had wanted to come to Texas. She visited when I was sixteen, but a month later, she returned to Pakistan. "Everyone's busy in America. People work or go to school. There is no family time," she complained. "This is not freedom to me." It was clear to me that Nano belonged in Pakistan or a distant Kashmir, her childhood home. She had no interest in living with us in Texas, a place without her stories or people.

After breakfast, Nano moved to an airy, light-filled room painted a pale, yellow color with upholstered cushions on wooden furniture, so she could listen to the world's news on an old television screen. She sat next to the side of the screen, paying close attention to the English news station. Surprisingly, even at her age, she could still speak and understand English.

"It's because I knew English that I was made principal of the school," Nano declared. "That's a rare position for a woman." After school, Nano tutored children in the evenings to supplement her income. "She was never home," Mama said. In their home, Mama lived with her siblings, her mother, Nano's parents, and a great grandfather.

As she listened to the daily news, Nano's fingers circled the prayer beads. I called them her worry beads. In many cultures, people fiddled obsessively with prayer beads or polished stones for spiritual comfort. This simple act of remembering God by invoking his name or repeating the same prayer with the touch of cold marble stones or round wooden beads can have a physiological advantage. In her book, *A Natural History of the Senses,* Author Diane Ackerman wrote of these worry beads: "...the brain-wave patterns this produces are those of a mind made calm by repeated touch stimulation."[10] In a large, empty house, there was no one there for Nano to hold, except the soothing touch of beads, which reassured her she wasn't alone.

I stayed a few days at a time with Nano. I spent most of my time traveling through Pakistan to interview and research victims of violence, study terrorism trends and examine security challenges until I discovered Kashmir.

With Nano's blessing, I would travel to *Wonderland*. Alone. There, I would witness the desire for freedom. I would meet people generous with their time even when worn down by conflict. I would meet women tortured, traumatized, and trapped by 70-plus years of conflict. Nano's childhood stories inspired me enough to step into a troubled land.

3

MILITARIZATION

"Kashmir is the unfinished business of Indian independence."
--ARUNDHATI ROY, INDIAN AUTHOR & ACTIVIST

"The history of India in Kashmir has been a story of false promises, manipulated elections...terror, more lies and so on."
--ARIF AYAZ PARREY, KASHMIRI WRITER

The city of Srinagar lay under siege by rebels, resistance fighters, and revolutionaries. A mighty military used tear gas, gunfire, tanks, and beatings to disperse a crowd of protestors. The Indian military's ubiquitous presence in Kashmir was illegitimate and unjust. The Army's occupancy and heavy-handed tactics against unarmed civilians enraged the Kashmiri youth. Participation in the freedom movement was their only option to challenge the Indian armed forces and protect the city they cherished.

When the city was calm, Srinagar became a tourist's haven. Visitors marveled at the deep blue-waters of Dal Lake, the *sazaposh* or hollyhocks and sunflowers inside ancient mosques, houseboats made of wood, and the moisture of the morning as spring swelled into summer. The sun in Kashmir altered everything. Even to this day, the beauty of Kashmir can be seen in its yellows—tulips and peonies outline majestic gardens; a cold sun beaming shades of gold on ever-deepening snow; and a tapestry of leaves from the chinar tree changing colors in autumn. *Kashmir is heaven enough.*

One of my first guides, Irfan Hasan (who everyone called Sunny), reminded me that Srinagar is like small-town America. "Srinagar is a familiar city. Everyone knows one another. For an occupied city, it is a source of comfort," he said. Sunny had shiny black hair, big luminous eyes, and a welcoming smile. His chiseled good looks and runner's physique concealed his true age. He looked to be a man in his fifties and lived with his sister and her children. Sunny never married. Over time, he became a loyal friend and excellent guide, sharing stories from a not-so-distant past and a promising future, or at least that's how Sunny viewed the world. He ran a business to make a living and often traveled to New Delhi, a city he liked for its manic energy and intellectual freedom. Sunny also adored Arundhati Roy, an award-winning novelist of *The God of Small Things* and a human rights activist opposed to her country's policies in Kashmir.

In India, few nationals highlighted Kashmir in the way that Roy expressed her disgust for the Indian State. She angered Indian nationalist parties and politician, who supported the valley's occupation. Roy criticized the Indian leadership for its oppressive policies and practices against the people of Kashmir. In Delhi, I found her books and began to appreciate her political activism. In one interview, she boldly stated what most Kashmiris expressed silently, "Kashmir is the unfinished business of Indian independence."[1]

I wondered, *is Kashmir India's worst nightmare?* A valley rich with resources might also have been a curse to the Indian State as it struggled to siege control of the valley—the long-term psychological damage of New Delhi's policy of control would be felt for generations to come. The Indian story—a biased historical narrative—is that Kashmir belonged *only* to India. No Kashmiri could ever accept this cruel claim. Some Indians agreed that Indian leadership acted with impunity; India's license to kill is unacceptable to Roy and others who understand that Kashmiris are unprotected and undefended against the authorities, including the Army, the police, and the paramilitary forces sent by a government backed by Hindu extremism.

On Kashmir, Roy challenged the Indian State, unafraid of losing citizenship or constrained by threats. Her position has always been that the valley belongs to its people.

> "For all those years, the Indian state had done everything it could to subvert, suppress, represent, misrepresent, discredit, interpret, intimidate, purchase and simply snuff out the voice of the Kashmiri people. It had used money (lots of it), violence (lots of it)...and rigged elections to subdue what democrats would call the will of the people...the well-endowed peace industry informed us the 'Kashmiris are tired of violence and want peace.' What kind of peace they [India] were willing to settle for was never clarified."[2]

To the Indian elite, Roy is stubbornly self-serving. Her once long black wavy hair had been cut short and heavy curls rested on her shoulders. Her slender face, thin lips, and deep-set eyes radiated when she smiled. She teemed with tremendous skill and loving-kindness for the Kashmiri people trapped by the spoils of war. "To the governments of India and Pakistan, Kashmir is not a *problem*," Roy wrote in *War Talk*. "It's their perennial and spectacularly successful solution."

The leading spokeswoman for freedom read like a great book. She walked with grace. At public forums, she spoke with tenacity and used powerful words like weapons. Her words were electrifying and comforting like a tapestry of Mughal art. And she always had a call to action. Armed with language, Roy focused on the rebels, resistance movements, and reform. She blamed imposing governments for crushing sentiments of self-determination, including India's policy in Kashmir. But that was only the beginning.

An activist, Roy challenged conflicts everywhere, including America's war in Iraq and India's economic battle with Naxalites, a tribal people in Central India. She beautifully outlined the Naxalites struggle to hold onto their land in *Walking With Courage*, written as if Roy were emerged in a deeply religious ritual.

Whenever I listened to Roy or read her writing, I expected something to happen. In a March 2013 interview for an independent news program called *Democracy Now*, Roy simplified the Kashmir conflict:

> "Today, Kashmir is the most densely militarized zone in the world. India has some 700,000 security forces there. In the early 1990s the fight turned intoan armed struggle. Since then, around 68,000 people have died and maybe 100,000 tortured...This is the crude end of it. Can you imagine living in a place where there are so many soldiers? It's become a very ugly stain on people who would like to have self-respect."

In a mimosa-colored shirt, Roy sat with her eyes averted beside Indian filmmaker Sanjay Kak, who shared his friend's revolutionary zeal. In his tenth film, *Jashn-e-Azadi: How We Celebrate Freedom,* Kak featured images not seen in mainstream news and presented facts easily forgotten. In Kashmir, there is an armed soldier for every eight civilians. His film followed the lives of ordinary Kashmiris as they struggled to survive in a place haunted by sorrow and secrecy.

Sitting next to Roy, Kak was equally impressive. A tall man with a charcoal beard and glasses, Kak was committed to revealing a misunderstood truth—Kashmir is far from free. He highlighted atrocities and abuses in the film and examined the changing nature of the conflict in his book, *Until My Freedom Has Come: The New Intifada in Kashmir.*

"The stone throwing was accompanied by the intifada of the mind," Kak explained. "For so long, Kashmir was characterized by armed conflict, but in 2008, the paradigm shifted. After decades, hundreds of people came onto the streets. The same happened in 2010."

The year 2010 was characterized as "the year of killing [Kashmiri] youth," as Indian state armed forces killed over 120 unarmed civilians. The death of Kashmiris sparked a new wave of protests by the youth—including young women—who took to the streets to resist the violent repression of Kashmir by Indian armed forces. The new freedom movement is one of Kashmir's untold truths—the long-standing struggle for freedom sparked a new cultural revolution that combined literature, films, poetry, art, and rap music to express the right to self-determination.

One artist known as MC Kash became popular for his songs, including "I Protest" and "Why We Rebels." In an open forum, Kash sang: *I'm the rebel of the streets that been eulogized in blood...Demonized in the news with their fabricated tales / While sodomized young kids are still screaming in their jails...They gave us blood and hate then wondered why we all rebels.* Artists like Kash formed what became the 'new intifada'—a reference to street uprising—to defy India's brutal military occupation. While the youth led the protest movement, women and men of all ages joined.

For decades, Kashmiris used street protests and other forms of rebellion, such as developing political consciousness through local organizations, to denounce Indian militarization. Together, Kashmiris were recreating their own multiple *histories* that emerged from conflict, rather than conforming to the Indian government's singular *History.* This is a concept I teach to university students, reinforcing the idea that war stories—the memories of oppression, sagas of occupation and struggle—originate from a people's lived experiences, rather than the perpetrator's manipulation of the truth. The occupier's story often presents the rebels as hardened terrorists, a convenient term used by the Indian State.

"Something significant is happening in Kashmir," Kak said.

Café revolutionaries I met in New Delhi and Srinagar confirmed the bitter truth; Kashmiris are locked with India and Pakistan's political and national self-identity. "Kashmir is the triumph of Indian secularism. The same act is a failure in Pakistan...it's the end of democracy in Kashmir," Kak said.

While Kak's films are like untouched art, Bollywood movies on Kashmir have reached millions. Indian superstars and self-serving directors have made films in the valley's foothills and along its lakes with dancing girls and hearty heroes. Most of these movies were sensationalist and stereotypical action thrillers. They were misleading and misconstrued.

In February 2020, Indian director Vinod Chopra released *Shikara* (boat) to highlight the exodus and murders of Kashmiri *pandits* (a reference to Hindu priests) during the 1990s separatist uprising. While there is truth to this story, there are gaps in the narrative. The film does not question the *why* of conflict: why young men turn to violence; why Kashmiris (men, women and children) took to the streets to protest a fabricated election; and why the Indian Army chose to infiltrate, rather than use dialogue and peace, to brutally silence unarmed civilians.

In Chopra's 2000 film, *Mission Kashmir*, the opening scene shows a *shikara* torn into pieces by an improvised explosive device. The head of security, played by my once favorite Sanjay Dutt, stars as a Muslim man whose wife and son tragically died. While the son's death was an important detail, the scene that repeated itself was an Army-led operation against militants hiding inside a houseboat on Dal Lake. The operation killed a few militants and the family of a Kashmiri boy, played by riveting Hrithik Roshan, who fought against the Army chief in an act of revenge. As the story unfolded, the movie exaggerated militancy in Kashmir with most of the plot outlandishly inaccurate. I could not imagine militant men targeting the holy mosque of Hazratbul, or a sacred temple to reignite Hindu-Muslim animosity, as the film suggested.

In another film, director Yash Chopra's 2012 award-winning and eye-catching *Jab Tak Hai Jaan* (As Long As I Live) begins and ends in Kashmir. True to Indian movies, the story was predictable and punctuated with romantic drama. The hero, played by Bollywood darling Shah Rukh Khan, defused bombs for a living as an Indian Army Major. One day, when Khan dived into a river in Ladakh—a region of Jammu and Kashmir that borders Tibet—to save a young woman, a sub-plot emerged. Though set mostly in London, the hero returned to Kashmir where he reunites with his first love. Of course, Bollywood stars didn't need a movie screening to visit Kashmir. To the charismatic Khan, Kashmir held familial ties. "I have fulfilled my father's dream by visiting Kashmir."

Most musical-like movies set in Kashmir revolved around romance. As a teenager, I remember being mesmerized by *Love Story*, a tale of stargazed lovers who desperately tried to overcome the border in Kashmir that divided their two national identities. Before any of these films, it was *Kashmir ki Kali*, an iconic movie from 1964 that set the standard when the legendary Shammi Kapoor sang to his lover in a houseboat on Dal Lake. Over fifty years later, in 2016, cartoonist Mir Suhail recreated the classic poster of Kapoor and the actress, Sharmila Tagore, by adding an eye-patch and pellet injuries to her face. In an interview, the artist said he wanted to "highlight the pain inflicted on this *kali* (girl) [because] there is no romance about the place or the people."[3]

At best, Indian films on Kashmir revealed its pristine, often untouched, beauty that drew visitors to the valley. At its worst, these films manipulated the truth of what actually happens to a people living in an imaginary homeland—a place in which their collective Kashmiri identity is challenged, crushed, and conquered by the Indian 'other.' Bollywood films distort the realities of conflict, focusing instead on family dramas, romance sagas, and action thrillers. While these films offer an insight into culture, they dismiss context altogether. And without context of the ongoing conflict, the viewer forgets that India infiltrated the valley.

Before the 1990s popular uprising, the cinema halls in Kashmir were popular. Kashmiri filmmaker, Hussain Khan, remembers when he used to skip classes "to watch the movies in the cinema halls."[4] During the 1980s, there were 15 cinema halls in Kashmir; nine were located in Srinagar city, including the historic Palladium cinema, once a famous spot. But after the summer of 1989, cinemas closed down "under the threat of armed insurgency after a militant outfit, who called themselves the Allah Tigers, appeared."[5] The militant group banned cinemas and bars in the valley and said it was against Islam. By December 31, 1989, all the cinema halls in Kashmir were closed.

A great fire devastated the Palladium cinema. For two decades, original owners tried to reclaim the cinema built on their property, but that case has been unresolved by development authorities in Srinagar. Situated in the heart of the city, the Indian Army transformed the Palladium into a bunker.

In May 2011, blogger Farooq Shah posted this:

"Beyond coils of shiny razor-wire and an eight-foot high fence of tin sheeting along Neelam Chowk, two policeman peer over rotting nose-high sandbags and into the street from inside chicken wire-wrapped towers. Some twenty yards behind them an aging, windowless stone building appears empty and derelict, its curvilinear chlorine blue façade faded by sunlight."

With the ancient cinema closed, the Army rented it for 700 hundred rupees ($11 dollars) a month. And the Central Reserve Police Force (CRPF) besieged other well-known theaters, the Firdaus, Shiraz and Naaz.

One morning, when the light was dreamlike and clear, Sunny drove me by the Palladium. "It was a favorite past time," he said, with an expression profoundly sad. Perhaps, someday, the cinema halls will be restored and reopened. As of June 21, 2020, Vijar Dhar, a prominent Indian businessman, is making plans to build a multiplex cinema theater at the site of the old Broadway theater, which was once shut down in the 1990s.[6]

Sunny was more than a guide to me. He became my teacher. I had so much to gain from a man with encyclopedic knowledge. He showed me relics of Mughal history in Kashmir, which included a drive to *Pari Mahal* (Castle of Fairies). He pointed at bullets in vacant brick houses in the old quarter of Srinagar. He took me to lunch at Kashmir's oldest restaurant located in the heart of Srinagar city inside Ahdoos Hotel, which first opened in 1918 as a bakery shop. Aside from the delicious local cuisine, Sunny said Ahdoos had historical significance to militants. "This was their focal meeting place. Some of them even stayed in this hotel," he said.

An intellectual with a love for literature, Sunny encouraged me to read the novel *Shalimar The Clown* by Salman Rushdie. "You will find references to Kashmir," he said. (In the book, one of the main characters' "mother had been Kashmiri, and was lost to her, like paradise, like Kashmir in a time before memory.")[7] Sunny introduced me to the work of Kashmiri-American poet and his only friend, Agha Shahid Ali, who earned his doctorate at Pennsylvania State University and taught at the University of Massachusetts Amherst. Ali was a celebrated poet. He won the National Book Award in 2001 for *Rooms Are Never Finished*. Of his friend's verses, Sunny admired what he termed the poet's 'immortal lines':

> *I am being rowed through Paradise on a*
> *river of Hell*

Exquisite ghost, it is night
The paddle is a heart.
It breaks the porcelain waves.

Ali died of brain cancer before Sunny could visit him in the United States. "It's the hardest thing for a Kashmiri to get a visa to travel to the West," he said. I wondered how many Kashmiris would leave India if they had the choice to travel anywhere in the world. I had learned that denying Kashmiris a passport to travel was another form of control by the Indian State. Those with a 'clean' record—individuals who had never been arrested or were seen protesting—were permitted a passport to travel to the holy Muslim sites in Saudi Arabia, for example, or study in other Indian cities. Few were able to come to America to visit. The passport was a luxury afforded to the few, including some separatist leaders who shuttled back and forth to Pakistan.

The more I learned about Kashmir, the less I realized I knew. "Here, everyone has a tragedy in their family," Sunny said. "You will find sadness everywhere." As an outsider looking in, I tried to feel his pain: the exposure to and experience of unmarked graves, enforced disappearances, torture, death, and detention were enough to cause a lifetime of grief. I wondered how Sunny was able to survive with no visible scars of trauma. He exhibited no signs of stress and instead, remained well-balanced.

You are wise, I thought. *You have a strong will and a business that keeps you* out *of the conflict. You have more resources, wealth, and education than others I have met. This might be the reason you are able to cope with conflict.* I was beginning to see that survival depended on opportunities *outside* of the conflict, as well as strong familial ties and a community support system.

Despite Kashmir's terrible events, Sunny and I smiled more than we cried. The more time we spent together, the more I began to question his decision not to join the militant movement. *Why do some men become militants and others like Sunny do not? Are certain people predisposed to violence?* I've had to answer these questions numerous times as a public speaker at conferences and other events. While there were no simple answers, I had come to believe that the reason a man (or woman) chooses the violent path is deeply personal. For Sunny, his father's influence and short-lived career as a police officer steered him away from militants.

"I believed a job in the police was the only way to escape brutality. I thought being an officer would help me do something greater, but in time, I saw that there isn't a person here who hasn't been beaten by the police or the Indian Army. My father told me I can contribute more to Kashmir when I use my mind. This is more powerful than any weapon. You need brains to outsmart your enemy," he said, pointing his finger to the side of his temple.

A café revolutionary, Sunny was charmed by Che Guevara, the guerrilla fighter, who forced the French out of Algeria after 132 years of colonial rule, and Russia's nationalist leaders. Above all, Sunny believed violence begets violence, a key concept in counterterrorism studies.

"Education matters...[and] we need courage to gain our freedom," he continued. Sunny painted a picture of Yasin Malik, the head of the original Jammu Kashmir Liberation Front (JKLF) before it splintered. Malik was poor but a capable and courageous rebel leader. Sunny explained that Malik's decision to "give up the gun" came from Gandhi's stance on non-violence. Malik's transformation reminded me of Sinn Fein (also known as Gerry Adams), the leader of the Provisional Irish Republican Army (IRA), who embraced a peace strategy with London in the 1990s after a long bombing campaign against England.[8]

In Kashmir, Malik was willing to talk to India and Pakistan to find a political solution to end the conflict. Other revolutionaries with political agendas were unsuitable partners in peace. "The clash between Geelani and Mirwais in 1993 created a clash of interests and a divide and conquer policy. We don't need to fight against each other or India," Sunny said.

A friend to Malik, Sunny believed he made the right decision to work with India and followed his example. During the fasting month of Ramadan, Sunny accepted India's invitation to tea. "India is making in-roads. I said to myself, if I don't go, it will annoy them [India]. I admit I would've been afraid to go earlier. My own people might think I am an Indian informant. But that day, when I broke my fast, I met an Indian commander who said I could go to him for anything. In that moment, I believed India changed. Look what time does," Sunny said.

One late afternoon, Sunny and I ran into each other at one of Kashmir's contemporary cafes off the main road in central Srinagar called Café Arabica. We sat together in our warm coats, next to a woman at an adjacent table with pale-green eyes and flaxen hair, writing in her notebook. Here, no one would interrogate her.

We listened silently to a mélange of music, Frank Sinatra, Amr Diab, and American hip-hop. Owned by a Hindu, Café Arabica became the go-to-place for activists, journalists and students. It was one of the city's few places where people intermingled openly—women could sit alongside men, with or without their headscarves. Or women could come alone, without being harassed by men. Like everyone else, Sunny and I ordered hot drinks and indulged in small talk.

"It's getting colder."

"I should be home before the blizzard," I said, half-heartedly. A part of me wanted to stay in the world's most beautiful conflict.

"I want to show you much more. There is so much to see."

"I hope to return."

"You must come back! Before you leave, you must have your last meal with my family in my home," he said, excitedly. Sunny lived with his sister, her husband and their daughters.

The next morning, I gathered my luggage and had the driver take me to Sunny's house in Rajbagh, an upscale neighborhood in Srinagar. His sister served me *noon chai,* also called Kashmiri tea or pink tea, a traditional salty rose-colored milky drink served with nuts, dried fruit and baked bread.

Back in Pakistan, I remembered an afternoon when Nano's sister, also a Kashmiri by birth, showed me how to change the color of white milk to a pastel pink. Sunny also introduced me to his octogenarian mother named Sarah, who had been a schoolteacher at a missionary school in Kashmir run by Miss Mallinson.

"She was a great lady who did good work to spread women's education," Sunny said, describing the English woman. "The school was eventually renamed after her." When Sunny's mother married, she stopped teaching there.

Kashmir cast a spell on me. When I returned home, I followed Sunny's advice and read Shahid Ali's poetry. I also read *Che Guevara* by Jon Lee Anderson, a monstrous study of the rebel's life. It helped me understand why many Kashmiri political activists plastered images of Che on their office walls—Che represented resistance against an oppressive ruler.

Finally, I browsed the autobiography of Martin Luther King, Jr. by Marshall Frady, which brought back memories of workshops I attended led by local journalists. America's prominent civil rights leader inspired Kashmiri youth: *So let freedom ring! Let freedom ring from Stone Mountain of Georgia. Let freedom ring from every hill and molehill of Mississippi.*[9] One Kashmiri journalist later added: "Let freedom ring from the Himalayan mountains!"

Since Sunny admired Arundhuti Roy's political activism, I picked up a copy of *Walking with the Comrades*, a story of India's "war with its own citizens...desperately poor tribal people living" in the state of Orissa, before they became forest guerrillas.[10] (In her book, Roy made several references to Kashmir: "Almost from the moment India became a sovereign nation it turned into a colonial power, annexing territory, waging war. It never hesitated to use military interventions to address political problems [to include] Kashmir.")[11] Roy consistently asked her readers to consider why India had "tens of thousands...killed with impunity, hundreds of thousands tortured. All of this behind the benign mask of democracy."[12]

I did what Sunny had wanted me to do. To keep learning, reading, and asking questions, no matter how uncomfortable they might make me feel. He encouraged me to engage both Indians and Pakistanis to understand their mindset. Even in America, the close ties I had developed with Indian Americans was just as important to me as my allies with Pakistani Americans—they helped me appreciate the diverse views that exist on Kashmir. Their lived experiences and personal narratives were just as important to the overall story of Kashmir.

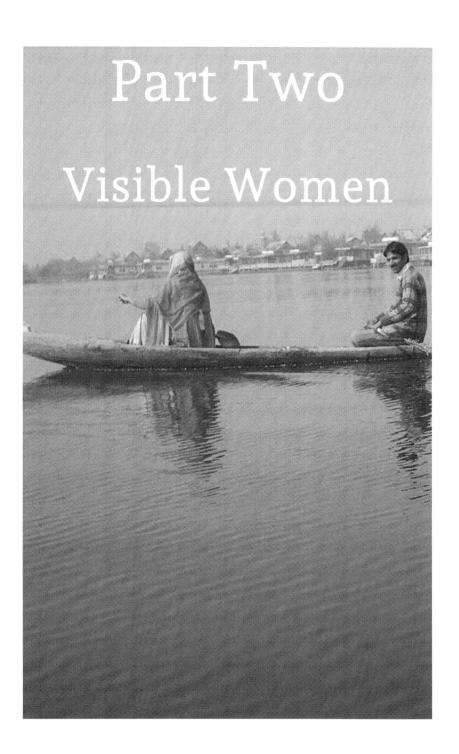

Part Two

Visible Women

4

BOMB GIRL

"If I cannot live, then I want to die."
--SADIA, AN ACTIVIST

"Personal grievances give rise to holy war."
--DR. JESSICA STERN, AMERICAN SCHOLAR

She had the most beautiful eyes. They matched her headscarf and *abaya*, an ankle-length Islamic dress, the color of pearl gray. A young woman I will call Sadia wore no make-up, though I imagined her eyelids painted a sublime blue and her hair falling over her shoulders. In a Valentino dress, she could have seduced men. She had a charming smile and a sweet voice. Beside her, I chose to loosely cover my hair in a blue teal pashmina shawl and sported a knee-length silk shirt and loose pants. I should have worn white cotton. Sadia reached for my hand. We walked together under the chalky sunlight.

In July, Srinagar is mildly tropical by day and cool by night. Flies buzzed haphazardly. The atmosphere was arid. Only a few damp clouds billowed. I prayed for rain. Sadia led the way on the wide road. Shopkeepers lazily turned their heads. The Indian Army on patrol gawked as we silently turned into a corner street.

"I volunteered for a suicide operation," Sadia said, her head lowered.

"The men turned me away. They said they didn't need women. But they are wrong."

Wait! Aren't you a Muslim? Doesn't Islam forbid this? I wanted to scream at her. I knew Islam better than this young woman raised in a Muslim conservative culture.

I tried to understand what causes an attractive, intelligent young woman to choose death over life. Sadia didn't look like a hardened criminal or terrorist. At first glance, she didn't appear emotionally unstable or mentally insane. But I knew violent women didn't fit any profile. A female bomber could be young or old, single or married, widowed, and have children. With more than a decade of research, the academic and intelligence communities have yet to agree on whether psychological profiles of militant women are a useful way to understand their drive to commit violent acts. What we do know is that common themes exist, largely reflected by personal grievances, which includes perceived injustice and the indiscriminate use of violence by authorities on distressed Muslim communities and individuals.

What all these women had in common is their commitment to a cause. For Sadia, the freedom of Kashmir was reason enough to strap on the bomb—a goal that suits her male handlers. Because of their gender, violent men view women as attractive and agile. The perception that women can mask her activities and disguise her intentions to be violent compels men to reconsider "hiring" women, even when conservative groups argue against it. Luckily, for Sadia, the *Lashkar-e-Tayba* wanted nothing to do with her—at least not now.

Still, I wondered. *Did I overlook something? What explains Sadia's motives? Was she abused as a child? Did someone hurt her? Did she lose someone in her family? Did she witness unthinkable acts of aggression? Did she volunteer for a suicide operation for herself or to prove to men she is capable? What does her family say about all this? Do they know?* There were too many questions unanswered. It would have been impossible to learn more about Sadia's childhood and family background in one afternoon. All I could see was her veil, a perfect cover for any anxiety, depression, fear, or bomb she might have been carrying.

As a result of an ongoing conflict, countless women I have interviewed in the valley exhibited signs of anxiety, depression, and trauma. They don't sleep. Some have nightmares. They can't eat. One woman lost her voice when she learned her youngest son was thrown in jail for a crime she says he didn't commit. Many women take common anti-depressants to cope with conflict. Others like Sadia seek comfort and strength in a movement. They are a part of something larger than themselves and wish to forget their individual grievances. Being part of a movement creates a sense of belonging and offers women a wider community, other than her immediate family members.

As noon approached, the breeze stopped. I followed Sadia to a shady spot. We stood across each other, leaning against a brick wall.

"The men didn't have to refuse me."

You have so much to live for. You can continue studying. Stay single or get married. Have children if you wish. You do not know what you are saying.

"I quit the organization."

Sadia referred to the *Lashkar-e-Taiba* or LeT, an extremist group based in Pakistan. In November 2008, the LeT perpetrated one of the deadliest terror attacks across India's financial hub, Mumbai. The reign of terror killed more than 150 Indians. Founded by Hafiz Saeed, who has a $10 million reward for his capture from America, the LeT is arguably Pakistan's prized weapon against a mighty Indian Army. Pakistan continues to publicly deny ideological, logistical, and financial support for LeT, a point that is still debated. Thankfully, India restrained and did not go to war with Pakistan, but agreed to a joint investigation. The Kashmir peace process perished and was then put on hold. In 2013, clashes along the guarded border further disrupted any effort to press for a political solution in Kashmir.

"I had no choice," Sadia said, her eyes to the black gate ahead. "I joined a women's organization. Women do two things: They stay at home or protest. But we need something more." She leaned towards me.

"I have to find a way to convince other girls like me that jihad is the only way," she whispered. Suddenly, I witnessed an innocent-looking girl turn to violence for a false sense of security.

By now, I had grown tired of Kashmir's secrets. In a conflict, almost everyone sheltered a secret from the authorities. A mother would protect her son from an arrest and lie about where he is hiding. A wife can pretend she doesn't know her husband is a militant. A daughter can forgive her mother's decision to lead a movement, making less time for her, and yet never fully understand it.

On the dusty road, it was impossible to know if Sadia could be callous, careless, or crazy. She had known me for a few hours and somehow believed she could trust me. I suspect she needed someone from the outside to listen and understand her. Sometimes, all a person needs is a stranger to show sympathy; someone to believe in and listen to, even if their secrets burdened us.

I watched Indian guards pace up and down the street, twirling thick wooden sticks, their primary weapon.

Sadia stopped and raised her head to the sky. A flock of birds circled above the roof of black-green trees. In the distance, they were like paper butterflies. We heard their cries. A natural light reflected off the girl's eyes, her beauty "an exception, always *in despite of*, [which] is why it moves us," wrote American environmentalist John Berger in *The Sense of Sight*.

She continued. "When I was 18 years old, I was a member of *Lashkar*. I was convinced I could be successful. We were planning a major attack. But the operation was put on hold. I don't know what happened next. The brothers told me there were enough men. They didn't need a woman to attack India. I did not expect this."

"The men were foolish," she said again, in a passionate display of defiance.

"I have a responsibility to my people. Do you understand?"

I nodded in disbelief. *And who would be responsible for your actions?* Sadia may have sounded determined, but she was confused. Her abstract emotions of a holy war that would alter the political landscape of Kashmir were fantasia. I assumed she had unexpected flashes of glory, a moment when she could imagine herself a martyr or a *mujahida*, the female word for 'mujahid,' the name for a fighter. The *mujahid* is a reference for hundreds of men armed and trained by the United States, Saudi Arabia, and Pakistan to push the Soviet Union out of Afghanistan during the Cold War. The early female fighters who defended their Prophet were rightfully called the *mujahidaat*, the plural of female fighters. Until Sadia was ready to let go of the bomb, she had no right to consider herself a martyr.

"The men don't see my power. They don't think I can do it."

Strap on the bomb? She made it sound like putting on a lace dress. Her unbridled spirit was enviable and dangerous.

As we kept walking, the sun's warm golden light danced on the rooftops of houses we passed. In a small garden nearby, flowers resembled luxurious wrapping paper.

"The world will know what is going on here if I do this. No one sees Kashmir."

I tried to understand what Sadia really wanted. She needed the world to take action in Kashmir and end the conflict. I sensed that violence was a symbol for honor, dignity, and respect. Terrorism was a timeless and often compelling method to force the international community to ask the pivotal questions: why does it [the conflict] matter and what do they want? My counter-terrorism experience had taught me that contextual pressures helped explain radical, violent behavior. The more I listened to Sadia, the more I accepted that she was a victim of a protracted local conflict and international inaction —these conditions explained, in part, her commitment to change the conflict through whatever means necessary. And by doing *something*, Sadia could believe she was part of something bigger than herself; she belonged to a cause; and her life had purpose.

There was awkwardness and a heavy silence for a minute as we continued to walk side by side. The air was stiff and a shaft of sun crossed the stone bench. In the summer heat, I could feel our physical breathlessness.

"That's not true," Sadia said, breaking the silence. "It's the only way."

"They do see you. I talk about Kashmir all the time. I teach. I write. Some Americans do care," I protested. I thought of lectures I had given. Or articles I had written on Kashmir, starting in summer 2008 for *Ms.* magazine titled "Kashmiri Women Speak Out" with Sarah Wachter. She didn't read *The New York Times* either, which chronicles the conflict in Kashmir every few weeks. To her credit, however, Kashmir remained the invisible conflict. Both its beauty and tragedy unseen and unknown to much of the Western world.

Those who don't know about Kashmir are not at fault. Many Americans are too busy living to care or understand a conflict they may never see or hear about in the news, in lands they do not recognize. Ignorance or isolation is not uniquely American. Most Kashmiris will also never visit the United States. Most view America through a diluted media lens that includes sensationalized television dramas and Hollywood movies. With limited access to a place and its people, it's no wonder that biases are born, and stereotypes are solidified. If only Sadia knew what I know about America—its culture, principles and values, but how could she? Sadia lived in one of the most remote places on earth.

"I want to be a martyr," Sadia admitted.

This can't be the way to Paradise. Martyrdom means 'to bear witness' and to sacrifice in God's name. Only self-defense was allowed in Islam. Never violence for the sake of violence. I remembered an oral tradition by the Prophet of Islam that rejected suicide: "The gates of Heaven will be closed forever to anyone who takes his/her own life." *Maybe Sadia didn't want to accept the tradition, or she was manipulated by militant men. There was so much about her I didn't know or understand.*

When militant men declare martyrdom, it is expected, even predicted. But women are rarely seen as victimizers. A longtime friend, Dr. Mia Bloom, makes a distinction between the victim and victimizer—women can be both. I had no right to judge Sadia, but it seemed unusual for women of Kashmir to choose death over life. Many women were educated and working professionals. Even Sadia studied at the university. She led women's protests. She had earned the respect of other women. She was already doing something positive. I wanted her to believe that. And yet, Sadia would rather die than live under Kashmir's current conditions.

Luckily, Kashmir did not have a history of female suicide bombers. There was only one report. In October 2005, a twenty-two year old Kashmiri woman detonated minutes before an Indian Army convoy passed along a highway in Avantipora, a town 20 miles south of Srinagar. Her name was Hafsa. There was very little known about the woman. Basharat Peer's investigation claimed she had an affair with a militant and ran home to join him. His study suggested that there were social taboos against girls, who married Pakistani militants, and if they do, they are no longer accepted into conservative, traditional Kashmiri society. The female bomber was a member of the Daughters of Ayesha, a woman's wing of the terrorist group, *Jaish-e-Muhammad* (JeM), another radical group based in Pakistan.

In the early days of Islam, Muslim women helped their men to victory. They tended to wounded soldiers. They carried messages and money. They called on men to fight to protect Muhammad. They were the mothers of the believers.[1] Women were skilled in warfare. They were given swords to use in fighting by the early Muslim men. One of the most celebrated female fighters is Nusyba bint Ka'ab, also known as Umm Umarah (mother of Umarah). She fought in Islam's second Battle of Uhud in 625 C.E., lost one arm, and suffered eleven wounds as she protected her Prophet.[2] After Muhammad's death, Muslim women continued to fight. A Bedouin woman, Khawlah bint al-Azwar al-Kindiyaah, dressed like a knight and entered the battlefield with other women. She "slashed the head of the Greek," a reference to the Byzantines who retreated after Muslims declared victory.[3]

But what these women did not do was abuse their status as the most noble of women. Only those who sacrificed their lives in defense of their honor, homes or honorary Prophet could be called martyrs. By Islamic law, Sadia could not qualify as a martyr for choosing suicide terrorism.

The jet-black gate is within view. It is the entrance to the women's organization Sadia joined after she left the terror group.

"How far is your office?"

"Not far."

"Follow me. It's a few more kilometers."

The sun bathed our headscarves. The cloudless sky promised more heat. We crossed steppingstones and walked towards the chinar tree. The sun spiraled through the branches like a kaleidoscope. The mountains in the distance curved down like galaxies over green rolling hills. The scenery reminded me of iconic photographs from Tennessee, where I lived as a child. Then, I couldn't speak English. Punjabi is my native tongue. Years later, I taught myself Urdu. I never learned Kashmiri. I was grateful most Kashmiris could speak fluent Urdu or English.

I stole glances at Sadia. There is something troubling about her. I wanted to know why she was different. *No girl or woman I had met earlier in Kashmir aspired to be a suicide bomber, so why now? Did this young woman choose violence, or did violence choose her?* Trying to understand motivations for a would-be suicide bomber is almost impossible. Most terrorism scholars make predictions on too few factors. Most make calculated guesses.

In *Women, Gender and Terrorism*, I tried to offer an explanation: "The reasons why women participate in violence will vary, even where common grievances are present, but what motivates women to engage in suicide terrorism is bound to be different for each *individual* woman."[4] I still believe the study of gender-specific terrorism is limiting and based on too many generalizations to draw conclusions. If I wanted to deter or stop Sadia, I had to get to know her.

At the time, all I could see was a beautiful young woman with a desire to act. She wanted something more out of life than a college education and marriage. She wanted to change the conflict in Kashmir.

"You are doing something meaningful in your life."

"I wish it were enough."

"God helps those in need."

"You can say this from America," she bemoaned.

Sadia was right. I can't promise a peaceful future when the Indian Army patrols the streets and tracks everyone's movements like an intelligence agency. We are never alone.

I imagined Sadia to be the perfect recruit. Cloaked in a heavy Islamic dress, she was unassuming and undetectable. She was less likely to be suspected and searched in a conservative outfit. The same would have been true had she dressed without a headscarf and in colorful clothing. In many Muslim cultures, women were prizes of men. Untouchables. Bloom argued that women with the will and capability to detonate "are the new stealth bomb."[5] Theirs is an unholy war.

When Sadia mentioned the word jihad, I began to think of what it meant in Islam. In earlier published essays, I described jihad as an act of worship. It is a living, breathing concept.[6] Jihad originated in Arabic from the root words *ja ha da*, meaning to strive, to struggle, to seek goodness over evil. My father instilled in me his liberal, secular values so that jihad was something private, not public and personal, not packaged with emotional responses to death.

Terrorists are clever to manipulate the meaning of jihad and avoid using the word suicide. They believe martyrdom operations to be legitimate, legal, and laudable. They have distorted the meaning of war and opt for suicide, their sacred act. It is the ultimate sacrifice for which they expect a heavenly reward. Perhaps Sadia believed she could gain quick entry into Paradise with an explosives belt. She would not feel the pain of death. Her body would smell of musk. She would dance in the gardens of Paradise, fatten herself with sweet fruit, and enjoy companions of her desire. The only thing she couldn't do is wish for 72 male virgins.

If, for a moment, we believe that male terrorists are rewarded with 72 virgins in Paradise, then what do Muslim women receive for committing suicide attacks? What are they promised? What do women possibly have to gain from strapping on the bomb? Nothing, except a quick death. I'm confident that didn't matter to Sadia. All she needed was to believe that she had the power to change Kashmir. My experience with these women is that some are coerced. Others volunteer. Each woman chooses terrorism for different reasons. No two bomb girls are alike.

Why is suicide an attractive option to some Muslim women? In August 2005, when I left the U.S. government before any major book was published on female terrorism, I gave my first presentation to the U.S. government community on this subject using my experience and insight from being an intelligence officer. Later, I briefed my findings to foreign governments and American officials. I believed a woman's desire for death hinged on multiple motivations.

As a young U.S. Government analyst, before the subject of female terrorism became sensationalized and studied, I briefed the "4 Reasons to Die" to policymakers and senior officials. They are: Respect (to elevate a woman's status in society); Revenge (to avenge the death of loved ones); Reform (to improve the lives of a community); and Recruitment (to call other women to action). Sadia chose terrorism to reform Kashmir, which likely explained why she joined the LeT.

Sadia's drive to kill may have been personal, too. A respected friend, Dr. Jessica Stern of Harvard University, wrote that personal grievances "give rise to holy war." [7] Her list, which includes alienation, humiliation and history, applies to protestors and political activists fighting the armed struggle in Kashmir.

Sadly, Sadia confused fighting for freedom with suicide operations, an illegitimate tactic in Islam. She could learn a lesson from Indian history by looking at the long list of women who fought against British colonials. Both women and men led the first armed rebellion against the British in 1857-58.

Waging war against the British East India Company, a royal courtesan, Begum Hazrat Mahal, entered the battlefield. She motivated men to fight. When she and her supporters seized the city of Lucknow, she declared her son the ruler, and then escaped to Nepal. Rani of Jhansi was another famed woman. Her adversary, British Sir Hugh Rose, said Rani was "the best and bravest military leader of the rebels."[8] In one battle, Rani dressed as a man to lead her troops outside Gwalior in May 1858. She died fighting.[9] By the late 19th century, few Indian women attacked and assassinated their British rivals. Two teenagers murdered the Governor of Comilla and were sentenced to life in prison. Other women tried to kill Stanley Jackson, the former governor of Bengal, and Sir Charles Teggart, the police commissioner of Calcutta.[10]

Why did these early women kill? Twenty-one-year old school teacher, Pritilata Waddedar, led the raid to bomb a European club in Chittagong, leaving behind a note to explain her participation: "I wonder why there should be any distinction between male and female in a fight for the cause of the country's freedom?" Those words reminded me of Mama when she joined the war front in Pakistan. "I wanted to show men that women can fight, too," Mama told me. In all the above cases, these women were legitimate fighters, trained to kill the enemy for nationalism ideals. They were *not* suicide operatives.

In Kashmir, women proved to be a force to reckon with. They were active participants in war. Before the British colonized the region, a Hindu maharaja ruled Kashmir unfairly and women joined men in large-scale protests against the Dogra king. In 1931, women "from a rough, lower middle-class warren of a neighborhood in the heart of Srinagar" sang songs of freedom.[11] Early Indian and Kashmiri warrior-women were the archetypal folk heroines. They were legendary and locked in popular imagination. Sadia was not one of these women. As an American Muslim woman, I had a responsibility to correct her.

"Suicide is forbidden. Besides, you're too young to die."

"Nothing happens when we protest. No one notices," Sadia said.

"You are doing something meaningful. You are a political activist." I wanted to report her, but I believed if she wanted to detonate, she would have done it by now. Something stopped her.

"This is not who you are. If you stay focused, one day, Kashmir will be yours."

She didn't need a counseling session, especially on an empty, dusty road. Soon, a thicket of clouds would shield the afternoon sun and rain the size of pellets would fill the streets. Sadia listened.

"You have to trust God to guide you."

"I need help from the men. Talk to them. They like you."

"How old are you?" I asked, changing the subject.

"Twenty-one."

"You can do so much. Youth is a gift."

"If you could see what I see, you would understand."

As we approached the gate, she pleaded. "Talk to the men. They can help me."

The men she referred to are male political activists. At one time, they were gun-toting militants with anger towards their oppressors. Today, the same men are politicians, protestors, and participants in the conflict. Theirs is a non-violent resistance. They have reassured me they can never return to terrorism. "We lost too many of our young men. They were arrested. Some disappeared. Some died fighting. Most died of torture," a senior ex-militant told me. He made it easy to understand why militants opted for a Gandhi-like approach. "Violence hurt us," he confirmed with a long list of friends who died in the early 1990s.

Sadia and I pushed through a large wooden gate that was unlocked. A row of houses the color of misty taupe looked unassuming. From the window, a group of women in colorful garb and mismatched headscarves were inviting.

"Please don't say anything," Sadia said. "They know nothing about me."

What would I say to them? The bomb girl is waiting for an order? Often, I've wondered why Sadia chose to speak candidly to me. Maybe it's true. Talking to a complete stranger can be easier, less intimidating. *Maybe Sadia believed I had influence over the men, and if I did, what would I tell them? That a young woman wanted to die?*

The conversation in my mind stopped there.

5

FEMALE FIGHTERS

"Where are the women?"
--CYNTHIA ENLOE, AMERICAN SCHOLAR

"If women are remarkably diverse, why are such a small subset of
their experiences featured in those stories?"
--LAURA SJBORG, AMERICAN PROFESSOR

Inside a yellow painted room, I met Yasmine Raja, a forlorn-looking woman in her forties dressed in traditional clothes (a full-sleeved long shirt and baggy pants), her head covered in a nutmeg colored scarf. She limped on one leg, a result of being tortured by female prison guards. She looked too frail to be the leader of *Muslim Khawateen Markaz* (MKM), the Muslim Women's Group. A political party comprised mostly of women, they are a new brand of female freedom fighters waging a battle for peace. Without weapons, these women use their voices and numbers to represent strength, hope and a possible future for all women in the valley.

I read about the MKM in local Kashmiri newspapers. The group's primary goal consists of reporting human rights violations and leading protests to call for gender equality and identity. In Kashmir's conservative culture and society, it was reassuring to see women join hands to oppose violations against their gender. Much like any other conflict, gender-based discrimination and violence intersects with women's experiences in war.

The war against women in Kashmir is a gendered war.[1] Gender-based violence is a topic I explore in my classes at The George Washington University. Sexualized violence is a common weapon of war employed by male-dominated security forces that degrade and dehumanize women because they believe them to be docile, weak and helpless.

Together, Kashmiri women are taking a stand against gendered violence[2] and fighting for women's rights. In doing so, women are reclaiming the Indian narrative and telling their own stories because their voices matter; their participation in the freedom struggle is vital to creating ties of empathy and solidarity with the men of Kashmir.

For far too long, Kashmiri women have been portrayed as the image of a stereotypical gender in need of men to fight for their honor and homes. This is true of wars in general—men will fight wars for women. Kashmir is no different, except that I soon discovered that women of all ages are more likely to engage the security forces when their men and children are abused, manipulated, and worse, discovered dead.

Raja pulled out a chair alongside a wooden desk littered with piles of paper and a vase filled with plastic flowers. A large window overlooked an empty road. The room was bare except for the desk and a small table in the corner that was large enough for a tray of tea.

"Where did you come from?" she asked, in a meek voice. I explained my reasons for visiting Kashmir and mentioned my grandmother.

"She is a Kashmiri? And you are Muslim?" Raja's eyes widened.

When I nodded, she flashed a megawatt smile. She called other women to join us, including her second-in-command, Masrat Maryam, a tall, thin girl with striking brown eyes who looked to be no more than twenty-five years old. The women silently watched me adjust my long blue shawl and fidget in the chair.

"You're not well," Raja observed. I tried to explain I just needed rest. Raja ordered someone in the nearby kitchen to make a pot of tea and bring yogurt with white bread. She guessed I had stomach pain. I continued to explain my research. For years, I had studied and written about women in conflict, including the violent women in Iraq and Pakistan—my first editorial "The Bomber behind the Veil" in *The Baltimore Sun*[3] predicted the rise of female bombers in Iraq after U.S forces were deployed to the country in March 2003. But I said that most women were not violent—they only wanted to be free, like the women of Kashmir. I referenced the women in Chile who took to the streets to oppose the Allende government in 1971.

"As no two conflicts in the world are alike, neither are its women. Some women fight using conventional methods. Few choose suicide terrorism. But the majority of women believe non-violent protest is the answer," I said, confidently. Studies of women's movements in Latin America, the Middle East, South Asia and the West confirmed my thesis that women had the will to create new paradigms of power. In patriarchal societies, such as Kashmir, men were key players—they had to believe in greater rights for women.

I explained to Raja and her members that men can manipulate women to advance their nationalist goals. When independence is achieved, men often push women back into their homes. Terrorists do this too. Women who joined al-Qaeda and its affiliate organizations were a riding wave of its success. "They were like mistresses of terror," I said. To date, no woman has taken operational charge of militant Islam.

Raja had a blank expression. Masrat, who sat to my left, nodded in bewilderment. *How do you know this?* She might have asked.

"I want to know if you believe you are equal to men in Kashmir," I asked.

"We support our men, but we know they have their limitations. They are in prison or hiding from the security forces," Raja replied.

Before she could explain, a woman entered the room, holding a large tray carrying a pot of tea, a bowl of homemade yogurt, and plates of dry bread and beef kebabs. The teacups and saucer were locally crafted, encrusted in a pattern of floral gold, similar to a fine bone China tea set. The women insisted I finish the food, a reflection of Kashmiri hospitality—they considered it an honor to serve a guest.

Unexpectedly, a middle-aged man walked in. He was lean, defined in jaw, nose and cheekbones and had a receding hairline. He introduced himself as Junaid, the only male member of an all-women's organization who served as their political spokesperson. He spoke with a fast-paced enthusiasm in a knowing voice.

"We don't want a temporary solution to the conflict," he began. "If we surrender, then the next generation will suffer. If we compromise today with India, then the real issues will not be addressed. We have to fight peacefully. We have to keep protesting. We have all suffered in this conflict. I spent ten years in jail. The Indian government violates our basic human rights. At times, they block us from going out to perform our prayers. We cannot go to the mosque freely! What kind of democracy is this?"

Like other male militants out of prison, Junaid was eager to share his experiences. He needed an audience. His back-and-forth style of speaking was understandable and I assumed he wanted me to know everything. He said, "The policy of arresting and killing Kashmiris is deliberate. It is designed to force us into solitude to keep us quiet. I can tell you I have never tasted India's great democracy! There are so many Pakistani youth who cross the border and are martyred here. Jihad is their right! Of course, we do not accept violence. We are a peaceful organization that believes in non-violence. But we received nothing in return! This frustrates our youth and the militants who refuse to lay down their weapons."

"You will find pain in every household. Every man or woman knows someone in the family who has been tortured, and for what? Tortured for peace? Have you heard of such a thing? The militants will put down their weapons if we have freedom here. India underestimates our will. No one can break our resolve."

Looking at the other women, it seemed that they had heard all this before. Junaid's monologue, packed with emotion, made me second-guess his non-violent stance. *Did he intend to win me over? Was he trying to convince me that militants had an important role to play in the conflict? What was his main message?* His personal story sounded familiar.

He continued. "My father was a militant. I was eight years old when he was arrested. I was a child of violence. I took after my father. I was arrested in 1990 and then released. I was arrested again in 1992 and served five years. The Indian Supreme Court made special cases against us. When I was released, I was arrested again in 2001, even *after* I gave up violence! I was arrested again and again. It is the story of my life."

"Why were you arrested?" I asked, naively.

"Freedom is a crime," he replied, with a fixed grin. As abruptly as he had arrived, Junaid stopped speaking and left the room.

Next to me, Masrat waxed on enthusiastically. "The authorities here don't want us to raise our voices. They want us to keep quiet. Many women are simply tortured because their husbands are involved in the freedom struggle or because they think our men are militants. It doesn't matter if our men are innocent. Because we are their wives, we are made to suffer."

Her words made sense to me. All over the world, I read reports of women punished for their husbands' actions or crimes. *Women bear the brunt of war. They are easy targets. They are victims, abused by authorities for their relationship to men involved in violence. Too often, rape is a tactic used against these women. It is intended to dehumanize her. I feared that soon enough, Masrat would talk about sexual violence and confirm what I already knew.*

Sexual violence is an all-too familiar tactic of war. In Kashmir, it is a silent (taboo) subject. Girls and women violated by the military are silenced by shame, and the shaming of women through rape or the threat of sexual assault is physically and psychologically damaging.

Victims are scarred for life and rarely speak up. In many cases, female victims live in shame behind closed doors and are thus, made invisible by a society in which men uphold the honor of women. It is the responsibility of Kashmiri men to protect their women from the anarchy of violence. Gender scholars affirm that wartime rape is committed to perpetuate the making and fighting of wars. In other conflicts, including Sierra Leone, Burma, Rwanda, women were no longer silent witnesses of pain. The women of Kashmir sympathized with other oppressed women and used political participation and protests to express global outrage.

"When did you join the MKM?" I asked.

"When my husband was shot in front of me," Masrat said, incensed. "I was a young bride made into a young widow. I know the horrors of war."

"What did you do?"

"I remarried," she said, smiling. *You are lucky,* I said to myself. *Most widows in Pakistan and other parts of the Muslim world did not expect to remarry, and live the rest of their lives mourning the loss of their husband donned in white or black clothing, depending on the custom.*

"I have a new husband," she said, proudly. "I got married soon after I was widowed." Her attractive smile and sensual eyes could charm any man.

"I am happy now. I have a home, two children, and I also work here [at MKM]."

We smiled at each other often. To me, she represented the visibility of Kashmiri women and the different ways that women experience war and life in a prolonged conflict. Women like her are *more* than caretakers of the home; the new reality is that Kashmiri women are everywhere. When tragedy strikes, Masrat and her colleagues take to the streets to call for justice. Women empathize with the suffering. Women make hard choices every day in this conflict. They are shaping the story of women by playing a more active role in the conflict. They are redefining the way women engage in war activities—their roles are multiple, revealing the complexity of their experience and challenging the question 'where are the women?' In truth, the women of Kashmir are remarkably diverse.

I continued to listen to Masrat share her personal story in a reassuring voice. The solace in her voice made me believe in a geography of possibility—that women of all ages could be a provider, protector, politician and/or peacemaker. That anything in Kashmir was possible for its women.

Unlike Masrat, her leader Raja never married. She was one of the few women in Kashmir who focused exclusively on the separatist movement—she represented the few with an unwavering commitment to the cause, hoping for permanent change through activism. In a traditional, patriarchal society like this, it pained me to see a woman outside of marriage. It was common in America for women to be single, unmarried—it is a decision no one questions, but in Kashmir, the choice to marry the cause is admirable and yet, surprising. While no one I would later meet questioned Raja's decision, there is a silent sorrow for women outside of marriage.

If Kashmir had been peaceful, would Raja have chosen marriage? And perhaps have children? Would her dreams be any different? Would she embrace the gender, societal norm that values family above anything else? Or is Raja "doing gender" by diverting from the norm? I had to admire a woman who chooses an irregular path. For Raja, being a freedom fighter was life. The cause was her family. These are questions I could not ask the generous and tenacious woman sitting in front of me with an aggrieved look on her face, the scars of conflict reflected in her eyes.

I turned to Masrat, who continued to tell me about her work. She documented cases of human rights abuses. She visited the families of victims and provided women and their children with food and shelter. In addition to her work, Masrat ran a school in the southern village of Sopore with 110 girls.

"We give each child school supplies. They have notebooks, pencils, and a school bag," she said, handing me a stack of photographs of children with their new black bags with the MKM logo.

"We do what we can," Masrat added. "It's never enough. One

organization like ours can't help all the children or women of Kashmir."

Raja interjected with a photograph of a child. "Look at this picture," she said. "This is a ten-year-old girl with her mother. She was gang-raped by Indian Army officers in Handwara," referring to a village. The picture of a child sexually abused by a gang of para-military officers would haunt me for days. *How could this happen? Why did this happen to a child? The pained look on the girl's face could not even describe the cruelty of the incident that stripped a child of her innocence, dignity, and the right to happiness.*

In another photograph, Raja pointed to a group of women dressed in black robes, making them indistinguishable. Raja and her followers held up signs with the word "Justice" and shouted slogans at the authorities, calling for an investigation into the rape of Shabnam Rashid that took place in November 2004. The incident provoked wide protests in the border town of Kupwara. Villagers from the area took to the streets to demand the rapists' arrest. Authorities responded by firing shots at the peaceful protestors.

In another photograph, the victim has her shirt pulled back to show red-pink scars, her face frightened. "Her body is completely bruised. The officers raped her multiple times to punish the father. They brutally tortured him in the next room after they raped her and her mother. It is not clear what the officers wanted from the father. But whatever they wanted, they should have left the women alone," Raja said in a knowing voice.

"On International Human Rights Day, we held photographs of rape victims, including this girl's picture, and protested in front of the world. We shouted 'stop state terrorism' and 'stop genocide' of our people. We shouted to the cameras. We wanted the world to see that rape is unacceptable. It is a gross way to punish the girls and the women of Kashmir. We are punished because we are women." Estimates of rape in Kashmir varied. Raja counted at least 4,000 cases since the 1990s, but that was a modest number. The humiliation and shame associated with rape explained why families in Kashmir (and elsewhere in the Muslim world) didn't report the crime.

"Many rapists go unpunished," Raja said, "and an investigation is rarely conducted. Even when a victim speaks out against the crime and takes the case to court, the rapist goes free."

The same was true for the rape of an 8-year-old girl, Asifa Bano. In April 2018, for one week, Asifa was held captive in a Hindu temple, "where she was drugged and sexually assaulted before being strangled and thrashed to death with a stone."[4] Six men were accused of gang raping and murdering the innocent girl. In June 2019, *The Washington Post* reported that an Indian court sentenced three men to life in prison for the abduction and murder of the girl while three others were given a five-year jail term and a fine for destroying evidence. Struggling with rape cases, the Indian court passed a criminal law in 2018, making the rape of girls under the age of 12 punishable by death.[5]

For young Kashmiri girls and single women, the stigma of rape also ruined their chances of marriage. Many girls secluded themselves inside their homes. When the shame became too great to bear, some girls committed suicide. The overpowering feelings of shame and social stigmas made these girls feel like 'unwanted' members of society.

Sexual violence is another form of reinforced gender hierarchy. The subordination of girls and women by male authorities is a *hypermasculine* approach that deepens social stigmas against local females, who are helpless to defend themselves against the victimizer. And so, war is deeply discriminatory and militarization is highly gendered. Scholars Dyan Mazurana and Keith Proctor argue that violence "as a strategic choice [is] sustained through the manipulation of gendered identities, institutions, systems and symbols."

Therefore, violence promotes gender exclusion, creating an unethical and unfair outcome for the rape victims. Justice for the victims of sexual violence is one way to correct the wrong committed against them. And yet, in Kashmir, the victims' experiences and needs often go unrecognized and unaddressed by the Indian State, the entity with the power to prosecute the perpetrators—a right granted to the survivors in United Nations Resolutions 1960, 2106, and

1888. These resolutions constituted and outlined provide gender-just reparations (such as a naming and shaming listing mechanism and a team of experts to investigate cases of sexual violence). Sadly, in Kashmir, these mechanisms do not always apply when the Indian State is in control.

Raja handed me the photographs, and continued to explain her commitment to protect these girls. "Rape is one of the reasons we come together. We led a protest the day we found out Rashid was raped to make people in our community aware of this incident. If we don't take to the streets, then the abuse will go on. No one will know. I have to tell my own people what is happening in our remote villages. The world should know too, although sometimes, I think the international community has gone blind. No one seems to care."

Raja's passionate response to abuse against her gender helped raise awareness. At the very least, reports in local and Indian newspapers highlighted crimes committed against girls and women. However, Raja demanded more than a news report. She sought justice for the victim and her family. There were no words to speak after listening to stories of shame and viewing images of abuse. I admired these women for their beauty, rigor and truth. They were volunteers, playing an active, benevolent role in the women's movement.

Raja handed me her file of papers and pictures. "You are our messenger," she said, with bright eyes. "Tell the West we are survivors and stoic in our suffering."

"I will try," I said, moved by the enormous responsibility.

"All we ask for is our freedom and the right to have a life, as you do, in your country. This movement *is* my life."

I placed the folder into my handbag and vowed to protect it.

"Will you be here tomorrow?"

"Yes," I replied.

Raja insisted I observe the protest she organized the next day. The women planned to walk to *Lal Chowk*, the center of Srinagar. So far, they had never made it to the city's main boulevard. The police blocked the road each time.

"Will you be arrested?"

"Probably," Masrat said, smiling. "We're not afraid."

Welcome to Kashmir. This is a place of infinite surprises, a land where the Army is the State. They are not here to protect or serve with honor—two principles an officer is sworn to uphold, as indicated in the United States' Law Enforcement Code of Ethics. Instead, Indian authorities enforce extreme patriarchy and chauvinism by using the Armed Forces Special Powers Act (AFSPA) to crush anti-nationals and so-called 'terrorists. How strange that outsiders (non-Kashmiris) determine who gets to live and die in a place that is not their original home! Most Indian soldiers are deployed to Kashmir from somewhere else. They gather like crowded moths around a fixed place, waiting for something to happen.

As the conversation drew to a close, I hugged the women and said good-bye. I wanted to say 'we will meet again' but this was probably untrue. As a researcher, I had gathered enough handwritten notes and a lifetime of lessons learned to understand—or in some cases, *not* understand—the visibility and invisibility of women in war. Later, I would question how gender makes war and war makes gender. I would wonder: *Why are some Kashmiri women visible and others invisible from society and political life? What do some choose to live gender expectations and others change the rules?*

I had learned and taught at the university that gender biases, stereotyping and expectations create boundaries around women; that some women, like Masrat and Raja, test these boundaries in a traditional society in order to write their stories of Kashmir, so the world can see them as they are: female fighters willing to speak up for gender inclusion, advocating an increased role for women in all aspects of life in Kashmir. Most of all, these are the women willing to die for peace.

At the foot of the stairs, I saw Sadia again. She waited for me, patiently, so we might speak again (perhaps one last time, as is often the case in an active conflict). I knew Kashmir was not my home, though I secretly wanted it to be. If I had my way, I would have stayed forever.

We stepped outside, the dust rising beneath our sandals. Raja instructed Sadia to walk me back to the JKLF-R office where the male hosts were also waiting for my return. Outside, a golden sky drifted behind a labyrinth of clouds. I needed to return to my temporary 'home' before darkness overwhelmed me. Nights in Kashmir were an "endless black, which seemed to stretch forever between the stars and even backwards in time"[6] that forced residents to stay indoors while the Army scanned the streets like flightless birds. The last thing I wanted was to lose myself in these dark, ghostly nights.

Sadia smiled warmly as we walked briskly. I prayed this young woman might find a greater purpose in life that does not include violent action. *You can create your own organization someday. Just like Raja, if you choose. You can be a great leader, blaze your own path. Was it possible for Sadia to choose life over death, beauty over filth, reason over insanity? God, I prayed silently, cast Your brilliant light on this troubled girl. Make her believe in a future for Kashmir.*

Sadia stopped at the entrance of the men's office and leaned against the orange brick wall. She held my hand for the last time.

"You must come tomorrow," she whispered. "I am leading the protest."

6

PROTESTORS

"It is better to protest than to accept injustice."
--ROSA PARKS, AMERICAN CIVIL RIGHTS ACTIVIST

"A riot is the language of the unheard."
--MARTIN LUTHER KING, JR., AMERICAN CIVIL RIGHTS
LEADER

Women marched. They chanted. They shouted slogans of freedom. Dressed in black or all white. Some concealed their faces with the *niqab*, revealing only dark eyes. Most covered their hair. Bright green headbands wrapped around their foreheads with white Arabic handwriting revealing the Islamic profession of faith *La illaha ill Allah, Muhammadur Rasul Allah* (There is no God but God and Muhammad is His Messenger.) The banner was a symbol of their religious zeal and a display of strength and solidarity.

The women looked like an undefeated army. Songs of freedom filled the hot air. In sharp tones, the women shouted:

What do we want?
Azaadi! (Freedom)
What do we need?
Azaadi! (Freedom)
What are we fighting for?
Azaadi! (Freedom)
Go India! Go back!
We want freedom!
Yeh Kashmir hamara hai
(Kashmir belongs to us)

An elderly woman in a Navajo white dress squatted on the floor. Her face looked worn. She held a large white poster with red letters. *United Nations, where are you?* It was an indication of the international community's betrayal, like a lover who had proved unfaithful. Kashmiris expected India and Pakistan to hold the plebiscite they agreed to in April 1948 at the United Nations. They had a right to determine their political future and decide the fate of their homeland. But the vote never transpired.

The women's discordant voices and jarring movements felt familiar. These women could have been in any part of the Muslim world. This could have been Algeria, Egypt, Iraq, Pakistan or any number of Western countries where women used the streets to grab the world's attention. One salient feature about Muslim women today is their increasingly active role in political and violent movements. Like their men, they demand the right to be heard.

"Protests are the only way out for people to vent their anger," one woman said.

In Kashmir, women protested when their children disappeared or died from torture. Like their men, they rebelled against what they call an Indian occupation. They used the streets to share their stories of the defeated. The women of Kashmir marched to send a broader social message. "Women defend women," one activist said.

In 2004, on International Human Rights Day, the women of Srinagar swarmed the streets to oppose the rape of Shabnum Bano, a 12-year old girl, by an Indian Army Major in Handwara. The women wailed as they held up the photograph of the girl. These women had a right to speak against evil, as the American civil rights leader Martin Luther King, Jr., once said: "He who accepts evil without protesting against it is really cooperating with it."

The female protesters fearlessly moved forward. I followed them, observing at a distance. I was a witness to an event that happened over and over again across the valley. The image of women protesting for justice, freedom and human rights is a common theme depicted all across the world. In January 1968, about five thousand American women peacefully gathered in the nation's capital to demand the immediate withdrawal of troops in Vietnam. In honor of the first woman to be elected to the U.S. Congress, these women were known as the Jeanette Rankin Brigade, and voted against both world wars.[1]

Another American trailblazer I greatly admire is Rosa Parks, a leading female activist in the civil rights movement best known for her role in the Montgomery, Alabama bus boycott—I had visited her museum in the southern state years ago. Parks triggered a wave of protests when she refused to surrender her seat to a white male passenger on a bus on December 1, 1955. Like Parks, the women of Kashmir demand to be seen and heard as they protested and refused to surrender to authority. Kashmiri women walked with purpose and fortitude, facing the Indian armed forces without a moment of trepidation.

The women exclaimed in Urdu, a language the Indian security forces understood. The leader of the procession held a small sports-type megaphone. I heard her thundering voice.

> *Go! India! Go!*
> *You cannot stay here!*
> *We demand our rights!*

We demand our land!
We have the right to live!
Go! India! Go!

I saw her eyes. Sadia winked at me. I knew she knew I was there, watching her call for justice and peace in a land torn by conflict. Her words reverberated through the air, like an ancient song. Her followers repeated after her, their raucous voices louder than microphones. Alongside her was Yasmeen Raja, the head of Muslim Khawateen Markaz (Muslim Women's Organization) or MKM. She was known to be resilient, patient and stoic.

Men told me about numerous beatings in prison that forced her to limp on one leg. I recognized her in later meetings and in protests donned in black. When she looked my way, her affectionate eyes smiled. I sensed her need to develop a friendship with someone like me, a complete stranger. I believed Sadia attached herself to a political group like the MKM for cover. Her do-or-die attitude endeared her to the men, who viewed her as graceful and genuine. But to an outsider like myself, Sadia was dangerously spirited and self-serving. She was a woman on a mission, and nothing would stop her from doing what she believed to be right. Although I admired her fight for Kashmir, years of terrorism study and meeting with other violent females proved to me that the pursuit of violence was not the solution to conflict.

The women moved together at a snail's pace. They wanted to reach Laal Chowk, the center of the city. "They will never make it," a male activist said. He stood near me for protection. "They will be arrested right here." Under the Armed Forces Special Powers Act (AFSPA), anyone in Kashmir could be detained. Passed in 1958, this act gave Indian authorities unrestricted powers.

Kashmiri novelist Mirza Waheed elaborated on India's catch-and-kill policy: "My friends, *all* my friends, went away too, and God only knows if they will ever come back. Not many do, you see, and those who do, don't live very long here. Because the army people, the protectors of the land, have decided there is only one way of dealing with the boys: catch and kill. *Catch and kill.*"[2]

Tan-colored police jeeps blocked the road. They were surrounded by a swarm of journalists and photographers. They snapped and clicked. Guards posed for pictures. It was an all-too-familiar scene for the authorities. No one was worried.

Female guards in khaki uniforms pushed the protestors back with batons the size of a baseball bat. The women stopped. They continued shouting. They were unafraid of detention. They were ready. "We will be taken. For a day or two. Then they will let us go." Authorities used temporary arrest to break the momentum, but the women I knew in Kashmir were unmoved.

Standing next to me, a former militant leader Farooq Ahmed Dar boasted, "Our women are strong. The Indians think they can humiliate them by throwing them in jail. But when they are released, they will protest again," he said. Dar believed Kashmiri women could tolerate unexpected hardship. These women had an instinct for survival.

Dar towered over me. That day, he wore a bright plaid shirt with matching blue pants and stood near me like a bodyguard. He was a man in his forties, broad-shouldered with smashing brown eyes, a Roman nose, and dark hair brushed aside. In silhouette, he could look frightening and a little anxious.

For months, I studied his profile. In 1990, a twenty-something-year-old Dar was arrested for murder and spent the next seventeen years in prison. Before we met, I watched Dar's interviews. He was the cliché of an Islamic militant: brute, composed, and strong-minded. Soon after his arrest, in a television appearance, a boyish and naïve-looking Dar in handcuffs told an Indian newscaster he did what he was told by his commander.

"I was ordered by Ishfaq Majid Wani, who was killed in an encounter and shot by the authorities as he was throwing a hand grenade. The goal was to liberate Kashmir...Wani taught me how to kill. He gave the orders. I would kill my own brother if I was ordered to...We are fighting a war," he said, coolly. (Dar told *Kashmir News* in November 2006 that his interview was taken "under duress."[3])

In Indian newspapers, Dar had been demonized and romanticized. One paper labeled him the "butcher of Pandits" (Kashmiri Hindu priests). When I asked about the men he murdered, he openly admitted to his crime. "That was the price for freedom," he said.

Everyone knew Dar as Bitta Karate, a name he was given for holding a black belt. And he prided himself as being the only one among his peers to have survived the longest jail time. That's seventeen years of torture, he told me, which included water boarding. In 2006, India's Tada court released Dar on interim bail, which denies him travel outside of India and stipulates a court appearance several times a year.

In 2011, Dar was anointed the new leader of the Jammu Kashmir Liberation Front (R), a splinter faction group, for reasons that seemed obvious to him. Aside from his militant credentials (Dar had killed more than most), he was a martyr-in-waiting. "I am married to the cause," he said to me one afternoon, as he leaned back in his chair, with a fisted hand pressed against his forehead. In the mid-1990s, when the JKLF chose to be a non-violent political organization, Dar joined the movement even while he was in prison. Years later, an older and slightly more mature Dar understood the risk of violent action. "Violence won't solve our problems. We tried it and we failed. Now I am a peaceful activist and this is the way to take back Kashmir," he said.

Like many other ex-militants, Dar is a self-style politician. He guides his followers. He leads marches. He gives speeches. He attends conferences. At the end of the day, when he is not arrested, he returns home to his family—he married an educated Kashmiri woman in November 2011 and they have a daughter together. On the surface, he looked like a changed man.

I could never decide what kind of leader Dar wanted to be.

The sound of the women became chaotic and loud. Dar and I watched the protestors from the sidelines, standing against the brick wall of an empty, old-looking building, watching the women tread slowly towards the police. Someone yelled, *"Allahu Akbar!"* (God is great) into the microphone, followed by one long cheer. Cameras zoomed.

"Our women are no different than men," Dar said. We moved closer to the brick wall. Shabir, an ex-militant and a member of Dar's organization smoked incessantly, as he turned to me. "These women share our goals," he said. "They have our aspirations. They are fighters like us. They are ready to die for a cause." The belief in a better life after death was a central tenet of the Islamic faith. Protestors were unafraid. Men admired women for being tireless champions of the freedom movement.

Earlier, Dar introduced me to Sadia in his cozy lived-in office of the JKLF (R), where men typically talked, smoked and dined together on carpets. Dar had told me earlier he would find a young woman to be my guide. "She will take you to the other women's organizations. Sadia will help you," Dar said, confidently. "She's one of us."

In a small way, Dar may have admired Sadia. She was attractive, conservative, and quiet—just the right qualities for an ultra-conservative man like Dar and his members. "Stay with Farhana-ji," he told Sadia. "She is here to learn about our work, so tell her what you do." Sadia nodded, shyly, her head tilted downwards. Dar didn't know

Sadia was looking for a more destructive way to change the conflict. He didn't know Sadia wanted his help. Sometimes, I wonder what Dar would have said if he knew Sadia volunteered for a suicide attack. In his role as a peace-loving activist, would he scorn her? Or would he embrace her martyrdom dreams? In a conflict, it's difficult to discern if anyone can really change.

At a comfortable distance, I watched female Indian police officers shove Sadia and Yasmeen Raja into the back of a jeep. Journalists poked their cameras into their faces. *Click! Click! Click!* The men watched their women being taken away. It was a chilling sight.

"This is another day in Kashmir," Dar said. "You have nothing to worry about. Women know not to cry."

Suddenly, I was overwhelmed and out of my comfort zone. *How long will the women stay in jail? Will they be treated fairly? Or beaten, tortured, etc.? Will they be released? If so, what happens next? Will they live to march for another day?* I wanted to believe these women shoved into the back of a military jeep would be let go. That someone would take them home. After all, they didn't commit a crime. They didn't use or call for violence. They didn't use physical force or hurl verbal abuse. They didn't carry weapons such as a firearm or a knife. They did not do anything wrong.

The right to protest to air grievances without fear of retribution or censorship is a fundamental right to democracy in the United States, and yet, this was not America. Even though the Indian State is coined the 'largest democracy' in the world, the Army suppressed forms of free expression, including religious expression, the right to a free press, and the right of a people to assemble peacefully to redress grievances. In Kashmir, the right to protest is dismissed by a dictatorial Hindu nationalist ruler in New Delhi. And so, without reason or rationale, Kashmiris were prevented from protesting.

Before I could ask, Dar gave me an answer. "The police will release them the next day. They know they can't keep these women. They just spend a night or two in jail. It's nothing to worry about," he said, half-smiling. And yet, I was discomforted. This scene before my eyes was normal to a people with years of suffering. Even the United

Nations Security Council Resolution (UNSCR) 1325, a historic security framework that guarantees women's rights, does not apply in Kashmir. (Note: UNSCR 1325 is the first international agreement to acknowledge and empower women and girls in warfare.)

On the dusty road, women began to disperse. Slowly, they put down their signs and moved in different directions, their faces like wounded instruments.

"They will come back," Dar said. "Our women never stop trying." The confidence of men, even former militants, in Kashmiri women to continue fighting for peace was unexpected as it questioned the old-fashioned roles women play in conflict as primary homemakers. With a twinkle in his eye, Dar seemed to believe—as did so many other men I have known across the valley—that women can break gender rules when both genders have a common goal; when women's participation is needed to break the chains of occupation; and when women give men more power, support, and strength to maintain the resistance.

In times like these, women's visibility is critical to sustaining the separatist movement and supporting the tactical and strategic goals of their men. Other women joined the separatist cause to lift their own gender out of conflict and believed that supporting women is vital to sustaining and empowering them. Both genders demand an end to the armed conflict.

As I was leaving, I turned to see a middle-aged woman facing the warm glow of the sun. She chanted softly, her body swaying to one side. *What do we want? What do we need? Azaadi! (Freedom)* The sun beat brightly on her black robe. "We will return," she said, in an ethereal voice.

Many years later, Dar phoned me. "Sadia got married. She moved to Mauritius."

Thank God, I thought. *Sadia may have a chance at a better future.*

7

POLITICAL ACTIVIST

"No jail can cuff one's thoughts or imagination. I will not let the good in me die."
--ANJUM ZAMARUD HABIB

She traded her name for a number. On February 6, 2003, Anjum Zamarud Habib became known as Prisoner No. 100 in Tijar Prison, New Delhi's torture chamber. The Indian High Court suspected Anjum of aiding and abetting terrorists and charged her under Section 22(3) of the Prevention of Terrorism Act (POTA). To court officials, prisoners, the guards, lawyers and security personnel, Anjum deserved to be behind bars. However, the brazen Kashmiri woman believed in her innocence.

After serving a five-year sentence, the innocent woman returned to Kashmir. Six months after her release, Anjum welcomed me into her home. A doctoral student at Kashmir University, Samie Shah arranged for the meeting. Samie had long brown hair, porcelain skin, and soft hands—she often held my hand when we walked the streets together or sat on a park bench to exchange notes on women. Samie was smart, engaging and compassionate. Her thesis-in-progress focused on women in power in Kashmir. It made sense for her to know Anjum, who she considered a chaste and courageous politician.

That November morning, snowflakes swayed in the wind like kites in a lavender blue sky. We treaded the road carefully, holding hands, walking past lonely-looking trees and distant villages nestled by glinting snowfields and bone-white mountains. We stopped in front of a charming two-story house slumped from thawing ice.

Samie knocked at the door. I had expected to see a war-weary woman with a hardened face and withdrawn eyes. Anyone who had survived India's Tijar Jail had to be brave or beaten down, or so the locals said.

Instead, a pleasant-faced and simple-looking woman with big, brown trusting eyes welcomed us with a warm smile. She sported a chestnut-colored sweater vest over a baggy shirt and pants, with socks on her feet.

"I've been waiting for you," she said, taking Samie into her arms like old friends. "And you must be the visitor." She nodded at me.

Inside, we were taken to an upstairs sitting room shaped like a loft. I huddled next to Samie under a thin blanket. We clenched our fists. Thickly drawn curtains opened to a valley with pea green forests, once draped with the leaves of summer. Looking intently at the view, I began to experience the fullness of winter in Kashmir, and finally understood what artist Cezanne meant when, as he painted, he attempted to capture the multiple reflections of a scene. "The landscape thinks itself in me...I am its consciousness," he once said.

After a month of staying in Kashmir, I had come to like the ground frozen and mornings suspended by an orange screen of light. Except for the wind that turned my hands into balls of ice, the season had its moments.

Upstairs, the air was thick and stale. Anjum pulled up a chair and sat upright, looking at us with luminous eyes. She had large hands, which she lifted towards her face as she began to retell her story in a heavy, soothing voice. Her story had not yet been completely written. Pieces of her life had been published as fragments in newspaper articles and online posts.

The story of Anjum's arrest in India read like a mystery. In her memoir, which had not yet been written when we met, Anjum's describes how her life changed for the worse in early 2003 when she was on her way to New Delhi. In the city, Anjum intended to apply for visas to multiple countries, including the United States as an invited guest speaker.

That February morning, she left the Bangkok Embassy and grabbed a taxi, heading to the office of the All Parties Hurriyat Conference. In her bag, Anjum had 50 passport-sized photographs, older passports she once used on trips to America and other Western countries, documents on war widows, and a large sum of cash. She also carried copies of financial documents with the cost of computer training for the children of widows in Kashmir, a new undertaking as President of MKM, the all-women's political organization she created.

The taxi crossed Nehru Park. A barrage of Indian police cars blocked the road. The taxi was surrounded. She wrote, "I objected strongly but just then two other cars, with loud sirens wailing, approached an IB [Intelligence Bureau] woman officer...forced me into her car and took me to the Special Cell of the Delhi Police at Lodhi Road." The police forced Anjum into their vehicle and confiscated her bag. At the station, she was humiliated, accused of being a terrorist.

The next few hours were a nightmare. A grueling interrogation ensued and lasted for hours. She lost track of time. She wanted to go home. She thought for sure this was a mistake. What were these men in uniform saying to her? As I listened to her story, I imagined the worst. Once, ex-militants showed me an album with pictures of young men dripping with blood. I was certain Anjum had been red, too.

She told me she was beaten, bruised, and tormented by a circle of men. "It was a soul-destroying experience."

"I am innocent!" she yelled at them. She had no idea what would come next. My mind raced with a flurry of open-ended questions. *Was this possible? Didn't India know she was a respected woman? Didn't India care about its human rights record?*

In her personal diary, an Indian inspector wrote down names of militant groups. "I waited, thinking they had no reasons to torture me. Torture is usually used to extract information. I didn't know anything that could be of any use to them. I was forced to sign hundreds of blank papers. I knew then my fate was sealed."[1]

The judge used the signed papers as incriminating evidence. Anjum was charged with aiding terrorist organizations in Kashmir. She was framed, and she wasn't the only one. In Tijar prison, Anjum discovered hundreds like her, mostly men, all held on terrorism charges. "They were innocent," she told me, convinced India mistreated Kashmiris.

Years later, she would reconstruct her life in a prison diary, enumerated with dates and events. She would record the greatest tragedy of her life in a memoir-style-book, *Prisoner No. 100*. We met before the book and her success as a writer in India, a country whose people remained curious and unaware of a conflict they had owned for decades. The few Indian nationalists who did write and speak about Kashmir were marginalized by the Indian State.

Prison dairies are rare. The first diary was published in 1975, written by seasoned journalist, Iftikhar Gilani. Anjum's book was the first prison diary written by a woman. In 2012, at the Jaipur Literary Festival held in New Delhi, Anjum featured her book with two Kashmiri men, Iftikhar and Sahil Maqbool, sympathetic authors whose own memoires offered a glimpse of life behind bars. Like Anjum, both men were charged with crimes they didn't commit. India, like America, did not have "a database on wrongful convictions" or false confessions, which often lead to these convictions.[2] Imprisoned for fourteen years, Iftikhar could empathize with Anjum—both served in Tijar Jail and believed they had a moral responsibility to tell the truth.

"Most Indians are ignorant of what is happening inside Kashmir," Iftikhar said, accusing mainstream media outlets in India for failing to report on the conflict. The Indian State often imposed communications blackouts in the valley and used censorship to limit the truth from reaching the public. In doing so, few people had intimate knowledge of what was actually happening inside the valley.

Each time Iftikhar tried to write in prison, his notebook was confiscated on at least three different occasions. He waited until his release to record the events from memory. Sahil offered an alternative explanation, "Educated people in India and writers don't go to jail. They don't know what goes on inside prison."

In Sahil's diary, *Darkness Within*, the senior journalist detailed Kashmiri prisoners framed for terrorism. "I was subjected to 15 days of torture. If someone like me [a journalist for 20 years] can be tortured, then what about someone without a voice?" Anjum agreed. She encouraged former prisoners to transfer their torrents onto paper to resurrect the genre. Writing could heal the artifices of pain, but more importantly, prison diaries could contribute to an understanding of the crisis in Kashmir to India and the rest of the world. In a stoic manner, Anjum told the audience,

"The government of India has not come clean on Kashmir. This is an issue that affects the world. We are human beings. We want to exist. We are not dead. We have not lost our individuality. We have not lost who we are. We want the chance to live in peace..."

In her literary narrative, Anjum vividly described the day Judge Ravinder Kaur called her a convict. "I was stunned. My eyes welled up with tears and my mouth went dry...The terrifying images of the impending five years of confinement in jail began to unfold like scenes from a film." The prosecution accused Anjum of funding terrorists, based on a tip from an unknown and uncorroborated source given to the police. The unreliable informant said Anjum had visited the Pakistan High Commission in New Delhi to collect money for militants.

In her book, Anjum described feelings of despair, isolation, and near-insanity. She lived for court hearings, which couldn't come soon enough. The book excluded scenes of torture.

"I will never share it because torture made me strong. That is between me and God," she said.

You are an unbroken activist, I thought. *Undeterred by the memories of pain, this woman recognized that she had so much more to give to her people—her gender—by staying alive.*

I watched Anjum fidget in her chair. She seemed anxious. Her voice was sharp. She spoke with high energy and enthusiasm unexpected for a former prisoner with indelible marks of physical torture.

"I come from an educated family," she began to piece together her past. "I am the black sheep. I couldn't compromise my values. A woman has to be strong. Don't underestimate the strength of women."

I asked about her decision to become a political activist.

"I love my country. I could not see women being exploited. I could not stand by and watch injustice" she said, satisfied. Anjum was grateful to her family, who prodded her to join mainstream politics.

At the start of the militant movement, Anjum was in college and organized a social welfare association for women that included Muslims and Hindus. As President of Muslim Khawanteen Markaz (MKM), she dedicated her life to helping oppressed women. "For how long will the women suffer the loss of their husbands, sons and brothers in silence? We have been suffering the bloodshed for over 20 years now."

If there was ever a quintessential secular woman in Kashmir who knew how to reassert herself, it was Anjum. Under the MKM banner, she offered vocational training for widows and half-widows. She educated them. She gave them a place to live. And she encouraged them to protest with her.

"We worked together for women's empowerment," she said proudly. "I didn't discriminate. Muslim and Hindu women joined hands until militants began killing Hindu pandits. Then the Hindu women left the organization."

To many, Anjum was a living martyr. But she was not the first to fight and die for freedom. Kashmir had a history of female martyrs. As early as 1931, women organized and protested together. In a hand-written document, Samie recorded the first five women who died for Kashmir. In blue ink, the list included 25-year old widow, Sajida Banu from Shopian district, who died immediately after a bullet wound. She was pregnant at the time of the military firing. Jan Begum, a 35-year old widow, was killed in a police firing in Srinagar city; a widow from Baramullah district died of a bullet wound after she hurled a *kangri* (a wicker clay pot with hot coals) at a police officer and disfigured his face; another woman was shot when the military opened fire on a procession of women; and twenty-year old Zoon Goor was shot in Srinagar when she led a protest. Unlike most women, Zoon was imprisoned nine times.[3]

Anjum idolized these early women, and believed she had an obligation to help her gender. "In a religious and cultural society like ours, women were not given equal opportunities, and yet Kashmiri women have made an ocean of sacrifice for the separatist movement." Anjum's feminist ideals seemed misplaced in Kashmir, in which men control the politics of women. "It's difficult for women to live in this political climate, but I have my own vision. No one can marginalize me," she said brazenly. "Not even in prison."

"They wanted to destroy my mind," she said. I couldn't imagine this woman broken. She was tenacious and had an enviable spirit like Rani Yashomati, the first Queen of Kashmir. Whatever pain she must have felt, Anjum knew how to mask grief with astonishing grace.

Samie and I patiently were listening patiently and holding onto a *kangri* until Anjum suddenly jumped. "You must be cold!" she exclaimed. "I can bring more blankets! You need more tea!" Our faces paled with frost. Samie and I curdled next to each other. Anjum adjusted her shawl and staggered down again. We heard voices of women chattering in the kitchen and a hissing sound of water boiling in a teapot. Within minutes, Anjum came bobbing up the stairs, holding a tray with biscuits and chai.

Outside the window, the snow settled. Leafless shrubs glowed under the faint light. Children played on a parallel street and recoiled at the sound of tanks. I imagined them running home, and then returning, restless for play, like turtledoves flapping their wings.

Anjum handed Samie a *kangri* that she held between us for an inflamed heat. The middle-aged woman caged her emotions. "You learn to live again," Anjum said with an infectious smile. I wondered if Anjum ever became unhinged. She guarded her emotions with vigilance, absorbed in the flux of her daily life. She didn't need to cry to capture the distresses of prison, nor did she need a spouse to support her. Anjum seemed happily unmarried, or perhaps by choosing to be single, she had married into the conflict.

Every time she smiled, I felt she was robbed of the right to grieve. In an interview she later gave to an Indian reporter, she said, "Incarceration can bind physically but cannot bind one's conscience. No jail can cuff one's thoughts or imagination."[4]

She continued. "In jail, I was called a terrorist. The guards and other prisoners teased me. Others accused me of being anti-India, anti-Pakistan. The other women harassed me. They shouted. They cursed. I thought I would go mad. I was moved to different cells inside Tijar. In Jail One, I remember seeing the stars and the moon. In Jail Eight, I was confined and couldn't go out." Anjum was never alone. Tijar had five hundred other prisoners.

Anjum carried her story like a string of monarchs. "When I was allowed to go to the court house for my first hearing, I saw so many men. I knew we were all victims. We couldn't help each other and now that I'm free, I've made it my mission to help the prisoners and fight for their rights." Her thoughts muddled together.

"The police sealed my house. They took everything. I knew I had to live. I had to survive. In prison, I learned how to stitch. I had to keep myself busy, or they would destroy my mind. I did everything. I worked in the library. I cleaned the bathrooms. I washed dishes. One day, the prison ward asked me to support a project for Jamia Milia University. They wanted me to teach Hindi, which I wasn't good at," she said in a swollen voice.

"At home in Kashmir, I never worked. I was the youngest at home and I was spoiled," she said. Instead, Anjum indulged in poetry. In her book and in lectures, she often included a verse she memorized in Urdu. Among her favorites was Pakistan's revolutionary poet, Faiz

Ahmad Faiz, a left-wing intellectual and Marxist. *The bitter, sweet sounds of the jail awakened / A door opened at a distance, another was shut / Far away as a chain rattled and cried / A key pierced the heart of a lock far away.*[5]

After each answer, Anjum stared in small emptiness. She needed rest but I doubt she ever made time for herself. "They [Indian authorities] have not seen my sacrifices," she said, in a defiant tone.

"I will never compromise. When you have a goal in life, you should never compromise. I will abide by my principles."

A year after her release from prison, Anjum Zamarud Habib founded the Association for the Families of Kashmiri Prisoners (AFKP). "Witnessing the pathetic conditions of the families of the prisoners, I decided that once I would be free I would certainly try to help them, which became a moving spirit behind the formation of AFKP," she said.[6]

One of her ongoing tasks is a survey of Kashmiri detainees in India and the valley in an effort to protect prisoners. "There is nobody to take note of what is happening in Indian jails," she wrote in a local magazine.

> "The protest demonstrations, press statements and memorandums have no impact. Prisoners need legal and moral help. I have made up my mind to take it as a mission. My heart bleeds when I call to my mind the plight [mental and physical torture] of my brothers in the jails."[7]

She continued to attend meetings held by the All Parties Hurriyat Conference (HC), a body of twenty-plus different political entities mostly made up of men, of which she is a member. "The APHC has been corrupted," she grudgingly added. "And highly degraded," referring to the Conference splitting into two different organizations. The split wouldn't make it any easier for women to be active participants in the political process.

In a separate interview, Anjum gave a passionate response to the unique challenges women in Kashmir face for joining political parties:

> "There is nothing written about a women's quota as members and in its decision-making body in the constitution of the APHC [but]... women's voices are ignored and their political participation and representation in the decision-making process is minimal."[8]

Out of jail, Anjum returned to her first love and assumed leadership of the MKM. However, the all-female organization she founded split into two groups because of individual indifferences Anjum had with Yasmeen Raja, who also chose to be single. The two women were free-spirited and independent, but had nothing else in common. Anjum stood behind secularism and Yasmeen adhered to a conservative, faith-driven ideology, leaning on a senior male member of her version of MKM for support. Both women believe they are the original members of the all-female movement.

"She is younger than me," Anjum said, which made her the pioneer of the women's movement. "I have made a conscious choice to be a part of the resistance and have no regrets whatsoever. Besides, I am not fighting against men. I fight for women."

While the worst was over, Anjum continued to be arrested for short periods of time. In 2008, she was detained seven times and usually released the same day. To the right of the open sitting area was an office Anjum ushered me into, piled with papers and unlabeled folders. Anjum shuffled through stacks of documents and photographs. She showed me pictures of herself leading protests, her raven-black hair half-covered in a sheer pearl white cotton scarf and matching *salwar kameez* (baggy pants and a long shirt) with large, round sunglasses. In the photo, a following of women donned in all black, some with a face veil, stood behind Anjum, who was the only woman in white. The contrast was striking. Her followers looked like moving shadows behind Anjum, the freedom fighter. She didn't look like a woman who spent years in prison.

"I don't wear the *burqa*," she said wistfully, "How can you fight in a full-length veil?" Anjum held onto pictures like old treasures and gifted me an image she was proud of. In a glossy colored photograph, Anjum waved at the crowd of women behind a metal screen in a blue police van.

"I will not let the good in me die," she said.

MEMORIES

*Mama with the late Benazir Bhutto, twice Prime Minister before
she was assassinated on December 27, 2007.*

As a university student, Mama debated men on gender-related issues and won trophies.

A Kashmiri woman in a pheran, a traditional dress

Mughli, the "lonely mother" searched for her son for nearly 20 years.
She never found him.

Qazi's lecture on Kashmiri women at Chautauqua Institution, New York

Local Kashmiri women silently protest, holding pictures of their loved ones. Photo by Imran Ali.

Part Three

Survivors

8

MOTHERS OF MARTYRS

"My sons did not deserve to die like this. At least now they are in Heaven."
--AMINA, MOTHER OF MILITANTS

"There is no justice. When our children witness harassment, killings...it forces them to take extreme steps."
--PARENT OF A SUICIDE BOMBER

Tahir was a frail looking man with a jet-black beard and thinning hair. He called himself a silent leader. "I don't want any publicity for what I do," he said. On the way over, Tahir gave me brief details of his life but no background on the woman he had arranged for me to meet. In a dry monologue, he said, "I was 24 years old when I joined the Students Liberation Front (SLF). But I was sixteen when I participated in the armed phase of the movement. That was back in 1988. Pakistan gave us guns and training, though I

never went to Pakistan. After two years, Pakistan gave us an ultima-
tum. 'We will support you as long as you take a pro-Pakistan position.' We knew what that meant. Pakistan wanted us to take sides, and
that was counter to our mission. We felt betrayed. How could
Pakistan think we would abandon our freedom struggle? All these
years, we believed Pakistan had our best interests at heart. Now we
know all Pakistan wanted was to control us and take all of Kashmir.
That would never happen."

"I was acting chief of the SLF when some of the militants went
underground and escaped into Pakistan. They were running for their
lives. The Army began hunting us like animals. All of our senior
leaders were killed in Indian custody. Middle-level comrades
remained in prison. I am one of the few survivors. I was released from
prison. And joined the Jammu Kashmir Liberation Front." (When the
group was first created, the JKLF was a peaceful resistance group,
until it engaged in violent operations and became known to everyone
as one of the most powerful militant groups.)

Tahir described Amina in sketchy details. "She is an illiterate
woman. She has heart problems. She is the respected mother of Hilal
Beig. He was a great revolutionary leader," he said. In a faded black
and white article, which Tahir gave me to keep, journalist Riyaz
Ahmad Khan wrote, "Hilal Beig with his revolutionary activities
attained such an international fame that he was counted number two
after LTTE (Liberation Tamil Tigers Elam) chief Prabhakaran of Sri
Lanka." (Sri Lanka defeated the Tamil Tigers in May 2009 after a
brutal war that lasted nearly thirty years.)

In February 1988, Shaheed Ghulam Nabi Bhat, the brother of the
famed revolutionary leader Muhammad Maqbool Bhat, sent Hilal to
Pakistan for guerrilla training. When he returned, he founded the
SLF in 1988, a movement for young men. Years later, Hilal was
arrested, tortured, and died in Indian custody. The SLF went underground for eight years.

Tahir had equal admiration for Maqbool Bhat, a predecessor to
Hilal. Maqbool was a pioneer of the liberation movement. He has
been called a rebel, revolutionary and resistance fighter. India labeled

him a terrorist. In 1976, Maqbool co-founded the National Liberation Front (NLF), the precursor to the militant group, Jammu Kashmir Liberation Front. He had a simple plan. He implored all Kashmiris to protest India's *foreign occupation*. He demanded that the princely states of Jammu and Kashmir, divided between Indian and Pakistani tutelage, be returned to the Kashmiri people. His vision was to create a secular, sovereign state. To India and Pakistan, Maqbool was a threat.

Both countries were not ready for a rising revolutionary and an independent leader. India arrested Maqbool and accused him of killing two Indians, including a bank manager. He was placed in solitary confinement and eventually moved to a high security prison in New Delhi. On February 11, 1984, India hung Maqbool in prison and allegedly buried him there. His death sparked a wave of protests across Kashmir. To his people, Maqbool was a great martyr and called the *Shahid-e-Kashmir* (Martyr of Kashmir).

In February 2013, his mother, Shahmala Begum, told reporters, "I have gone through terrible times during these 29 years. However, we must understand that freedom comes at a cost. It demands sacrifices. I gave my four sons to the freedom struggle."[1]

In honor of Maqbool, Tahir gifted me an Urdu-language book. "I wrote this in prison," he said. "I'm not a scholar. But I wanted the world to know what Maqbool did for Kashmir. I want the next generation of Kashmiris to appreciate his sacrifice for the cause of freedom."

When the car stopped, Tahir and I ascended a dirt road until he recognized the dark wooden front door. When it opened, a child appeared. "Go bring your grandmother," Tahir said. "We have someone here from America. Tell her it's important." I was puzzled. *She wasn't expecting me? What if she was busy, sick or away?* I stood behind Tahir in silence, waiting for the woman to appear.

Somehow, Tahir knew she would be there. A small, fair-skinned woman with eyes of a sheep and heavy lines etched across her face hobbled towards the door. Her plump figure was cloaked in a *pheran*, a long loose gown made of wool, her hair tied back in a bridal white scarf. Her arms swung under the heavy cloth like the branches of an aging tree. Amina greeted Tahir with warm, melancholic eyes. "There's someone here to see you," he said. "She came from a faraway place to meet you."

"Come. You are most welcome," she said, looking at me with limpid eyes. She stepped back as we entered. We followed through a long hallway until we reached an airy bright room the color of butterscotch. There was no furniture, only a musty rug and flowery cushions against the wall. Amina summoned a female relative to bring hot tea and *kangri*. Amina held it under her *pheran* and I thought it might set her dress on fire. I held mine at a safe distance and took cover under thick blankets on the floor to shield myself from the frigid air. I suspected the winter chill leaked through the high windows on the wall. A child who looked five leaned against the doorway. Large golden bronze eyes stared right at me.

"Tell us about your son, Hilal," Tahir said, as he looked down at his feet, remembering his friend. Amina sat silently. She uttered a few words at a time. Tahir translated the conversation to me in Urdu. Amina spoke in Kashmiri. "I saw my son come and go. He said he was going to New Delhi as a tourist. He was gone for three and half months. I found out later he was in Pakistan," she said and then took a long pause. Tahir pressed her to say more. "He came home for short periods and then disappeared for months. I assumed he was working," she said, with regret. It wasn't hard to understand how a mother could know so little about her children.

"She didn't know the truth about Hilal," Tahir said to me in a language Amina didn't understand. "For the first three years, I didn't know what he was doing or where he went," Amina said. When the police came looking for him, she learned that he was in danger. She knew he was a separatist leader. "Both of my sons escaped. During that time, my husband died. I was alone in the world." Amina told me she has two brothers and one sister. She asked the male family members for money, but no one was willing to help her. "My relatives were afraid to talk to me," she said. With Hilal in prison and two sons on the run, she had nowhere to go.

On July 17, 1996, Hilal died in a prison in Srinagar. "I was horrified when I saw his dead body. My heart broke. He was a part of my body. He was covered in blood. His fingers and hands were cut. His feet were amputated. His teeth were broken. His back was burned. He did not look like my son." Third degree torture marks were common to Kashmiri prisoners. Amina's eyes filled with sadness. "I have cried so much. I have no tears left," she said. Tahir turned to me and said, "She's lucky she did not go blind with grief."

After Hilal's death, her son Mohammad crossed the border into Pakistan. She believed it was the only thing he could do to stay alive, but suspected his arrest by the Pakistani Army. The small, heavy-set woman pushed herself off the cushion and asked that we wait. When she returned, she had a copy of a letter addressed to then-President of Pakistan, General Pervez Musharraf. The letter, dated January 8, 2008, stated the following:

"I am Amina Bano 75 years of age...from Allochi Bagh Srinagar, Kashmir writing you this letter. I had three sons: two of them killed by the Indian Army, and a third, whose name is Muhammad Hussein Beig, is, perhaps, in Muzaffarabad jail in Pakistan. I do not know his whereabouts but solid rumors are that he has been arrested at the instance of one of our relatives who is head of a Kashmir based organization there...It is requested that his whereabouts may please be known to me. He left me six years ago because the Indian Army used to raid my house and harass my family, including widows and children of my martyred sons also to my living son, now missing. I have a lot of hope that you will take necessary action in this matter."

She sent a copy of the letter to the Prime Minister of Azad Kashmir in Pakistan and the Pakistani Ambassador in New Delhi. No one replied.

Nearly twenty years after Hilal's death, Amina continued to have tremors. "It is miserable to live with heart pain. My sons did not deserve to die like this. At least now they are in Heaven. One day, I will see them again," she said.

Meeting the mother of martyrs made me think about countless other women in Kashmir, who had lost their sons to militancy. *How many young men would choose violence? How many more would die for Kashmir?* I wondered. Like Amina's sons, Kashmir's martyrs were revered for fighting the occupation. On his Facebook page, the once-famed youth leader, Maqbool Bhatt, posted: "My only crime is that I have rebelled against slavery, oppression, poverty, ignorance and exploitation of my people."

As the Indian occupation continued, the youth increasingly joined the militant movement. Many experienced the barbarity of war: extended curfews, school closures, communication bans, lockdowns, random house-raids and attacks by Indian security forces. For some, the only way *out* of the current conflict was through violent action.

As a counter-terrorism expert and educator, I examine the reasons *why* individuals choose violence. Their motives vary and include a combination of: altruism and adventurism; an identity crisis; social and political injustices; the glory of martyrdom; and much more. While the reasons differ for each individual, one thing is clear: militants are made, not born.

In Kashmir, ongoing human rights abuses and an endless torrent of violence is a valid justification. As more young men become militants, and die as martyrs (i.e., killed by Indian forces), others will follow. In 2018, a police commander said, "I'll be honest. For every militant we kill, more are joining."[2]

What triggers violence? Is there a single event? When I give lectures, these are the questions I ask my audiences to consider when trying to understand the context of violence. *What is happening in Kashmir to create an uptick in militant recruitment?* In 2016, a new generation of Kashmiris turned to armed rebellion. Many of the new recruits came from South Kashmir,[3] including Burhan Wani, whose death sparked mass resistance.[4]

On July 8, 2016, Burhan Wani, the 22-year old militant leader, was killed by Indian security forces during an armed clash. More than 300 people attended his funeral to collectively mourn the loss of a young man, "who witnessed oppression [by the Indian State] for the last 60 years."[5] Overnight, Burhan became the poster boy for the freedom struggle and his death revived the revolution.

Before his death, Burhan was "a normal schoolboy whose father wanted him to be a doctor and see patients for free on Sundays."[6] As a child, he grew up during the 2008 and 2010 uprisings, and like other Kashmiri youth, he was raised under occupation. The son of a school principal, Burhan came from an affluent family, and then sacrificed it all when he joined the militancy. To the Kashmiri youth, Burhan represented a new kind of fighter: one who was educated and wealthy, rather than the stereotypical poor and uneducated militant.

The pervasive hopelessness for Kashmiri youth and the abuse against them by the Indian security forces likely compelled Burhan to choose violence. In 2010, the episodic event that changed his life took place when Burhan was fifteen-years old. One day, as Burhan and his elder brother, Khalid Muzaffar Wani, went out for a bike ride, Indian troops ordered them to buy cigarettes and then beat them without provocation. Khalid was left unconscious, while Burhan escaped, shouting, "I will take revenge for this."[7]

Two weeks later, Burhan ran away from home, never to return. He disappeared into the jungles of South Kashmir to join the militant group, *Hizbul Mujahideen* (HuM), and he became "one of the most successful and wanted militants in Kashmir."[8] In 2013, the death of the HuM leader gave Burhan the opportunity to direct attacks against Indian security forces as well as continue the use of social media to encourage other young men to support the revolution and boycott India. In one video, he declared: "We should unite for the sake of our motherland."[9]

His elder brother, Khalid, did not join the violent movement and continued his postgraduate studies in economics until April 13, 2015, when he was killed by the Indian Army in the forests of Tral.[10] At the time of his death, the Army labeled Khalid a militant and said he was killed in an "encounter," a reference to a battle between militants and the military. The family denied the charges and believed their eldest son was tortured.

A year later, in 2016, the Army killed Burhan. The death of the young militant leader "triggered protests...on a very large and unprecedented scale throughout the Kashmir Valley and in districts of Jammu," according to a report by the United Nations High Commissioner for Human Rights.[11] The protests included "more young, middle-class Kashmiris, [and] females who do not appear to have been participating in the past."[12] The inclusion and acceptance of more women on the streets to protest the unfair and unethical tactics of the Indian security forces changed the idea of the innocent, helpless woman. As the conflict continued, women became *more* visible and proved that they were no longer confined to traditional gender roles. Their increased participation has forced outsiders to look at the Kashmiri conflict through gender-neutral lens.

In response to mass protests, the Indian authorities used excessive force, "which led to casualties and a wide range of alleged related human rights violations throughout the summer of 2016 and into 2018."[13] The Army killed an unprecedented number of civilians, and Burhan's death continued to inspire other local Kashmiris to pursue violence in retaliation for the military's rampant abuse. After Burhan's death, more young men joined the rebellion and they arguably became more violent.

On February 14, 2019, a suicide bomber, twenty-year-old Adil Dar, rammed his explosives-laden car into a bus transporting Indian soldiers, killing himself and 42 paramilitary troops.[14] This was the second-time in Kashmir's 30-year history that a local boy "had blown himself up while targeting Indian forces."

The boy's mother, forty-year-old Hamida, had not expected her son to join a rebel group. "I did not have a daughter. He helped me in home chores. He worked hard and was a big fan of cricket...He would burst crackers when India would win," she told *Al Jazeera*.[15] Without warning, Adil—like Burhan and other young men—left home. Hamida searched for her son for a month, waited for him, but he never returned. "I left it to God," she said. The boy's father told reporters that his son joined the militancy because of *zulm*, or oppression, which is forcing Kashmiri youth to pick up guns.[16]

Why were Burhan and Adil celebrated militants? An American activist for Kashmir, who wished to be unnamed, believed local residents harbored a love-and-hate relationship for militants. Even though most Kashmiris disapproved of violent action, they understood why men like Burhan and Adil turned to violence—it was a way of protesting decades of state-imposed violence against them. One resident stated, "There is no justice. When our children witness harassment, killings and maiming, it forces them to take extreme steps."[17]

Today, the youth are increasingly vocal and assertive in their struggle for political freedom and their demand for human security. Together, young men and women are creating a new story that includes years of broken promises and the denial of democracy—the youth will not allow their voices to be silenced. Their story includes thousands killed, and many more who "continue to languish in jails."[18]

As more young people die, I think of how their families live with pained hearts. The loss of a child is unbearable and unthinkable, and yet, mothers I have met understand the circumstances surrounding their sons' rebellion. These women accept that their children will continue fighting to restore their shattered identity, using violent or non-violent means, to demand peace and a political solution to the decades-old conflict.

Kashmiri women, with whom I have regular contact with today, only want peace and an uncomplicated life. They hold onto the memories of their fallen martyrs—hundreds of innocent Kashmiri children, including fourteen-year-old Tufail Mattoon, who was shot in the head on June 11, 2010 with a tear-gas canister while playing in a downtown park in Srinagar. Another teenager, whose name is not provided, was shot by Indian forces in "accidental fire" in his village while playing cricket with his friends. I learned of his death from one of my contacts, who was in the park with him. Countless other boys and girls have been killed as they played outside or walked to school.[19] This is a tragic and common story of children dying—the Indian forces do not apologize, pay for funeral costs, or visit the families of the deceased.

Today, the stories of martyrs are kept alive with "virtual forms of memorialization...[to] forge new understandings of truth, faith, death, and sacrifice."[20] Practices of remembrance give outsiders access to Kashmir's evolving history[21] and draws attention to the 'forever conflict.' For the mothers of martyrs, their boys have lost their childhood fighting for freedom.

9

GUARDIAN

"I would hug his grave."
--MUGLI, MOTHER OF MISSING SON

Zahoor led the way. I trailed behind, zigzagging through a labyrinth of narrow alleys. In the dense downtown area of Habba Kadal lived a woman, coined the "lonely mother."[1] "You must meet her," Zahoor said. "She is like a mother to me." The air was thick with frost. The sky overhead was black. In Kashmir, candles replaced street lamps. Soft light flickered through windowpanes. Zahoor turned around, "Be careful. Don't fall." I looked at the ground. Mounds of snow from the winter's storm were as hard as bricks.

Twenty-three old Zahoor was one of the most compassionate journalists in Srinagar. "My family wanted me to be a doctor, but I love literature. I failed the medical exam," he said, a cigarette dangling in his right hand. "I wanted to be a writer." Together, we read Pablo Neruda, the famed Chilean poet. Zahoor had wavy almond-colored hair, a medium build, and comforting eyes. "It's here, somewhere," he murmured. None of the houses were marked. There were no signs. No names or numbers. I didn't know how Zahoor was going to find Mughli, whose name faintly sounded like Disney's *Jungle Book* character, Mowgli.

Zahoor spotted an open window. "Hello!" he yelled. "Is anyone there?" A man's face appeared. Zahoor asked where he could find Mughli. He knocked on more doors. We wandered through a maze of houses and pitch-black alleys. "Don't worry. We're almost there," he said reassuringly. I watched Zahoor with zeal. We scurried through the snow until he spotted the large house. "This is it," he said, smiling widely as he quickened his stride.

Standing behind him, Zahoor yelled the old woman's name, his voice reverberating in the moonless night. "She's hard of hearing," he said. He shouted again, a heavy voice filled the air like church bells. We waited like rebels in the cloaked night. "Who's there?" a melodious voice responded. "Is that you, my son?" she asked. "Hardly anyone comes to see her," Zahoor turned to me. "Except me." "It's me!" he exclaimed with excitement. The sound of ramshackle against a deteriorating door was like fireworks in the night.

A beautiful woman with a striking resemblance to Nano greeted Zahoor with a warm hug and an exchange of sweet words. She looked at me inquisitively. Mughli wore a cardamom colored *pheran* and a starch white *pooch* over her head, her neck visible like a lizard's elbow. Round gold earrings dangled on her ear lobes and black-rimmed eyeglasses perched on her nose. She had a gentle-looking face, a Roman nose, and eyes like black pearls. She almost looked happy.

We walked through the large courtyard and followed Mughli up white winding steps. She lived alone in the spacious house. Stately rooms were visibly vacant and needed to be renovated. Mughli cornered herself upstairs in the kitchen. The walls were painted a turquoise color. Wooden beams supported the ceiling. Along a side-wall, small copper and steel pots rested on a gas makeshift stove. The gas cylinder stained with red and black paint was all she needed to heat water or cook a simple meal of rice and vegetables. She had no refrigerator, no fruit basket and no sight of grains. The ward-robed sized kitchen was disturbingly empty. Blankets striped in Christmas colors were piled against the wall. A glaring light from a bulb hung above our heads and a few candles burned frantically as a slow wind chilled the room.

We sat on a floor with thin mats. Zahoor told me she had everything right here. "My nephew's wife is waiting for me to die," Mughli said. "So she can claim this house." She lived in her father's house, where her son, Nazir Ahmad Teli, was born. His bedroom was on the floor above. Mughli kept it locked.

Mughli spoke in her native Kashmiri. Zahoor translated for me, alternating between Urdu and English. "She's very poetic," he said. "She said your dark eyes shame the moon." Mughli reached for my hand. She touched my face. She stroked my cheeks. She assumed the role of a grandmother. "She said you look like a local girl," he said. I was warmed by Mughli's compassionate words and graceful gestures. She had accepted me as one of her own.

Conflicting thoughts about love, war, women, and religion resurfaced. As I witnessed Mughli watch me, I was reminded of military mothers in America who waited for their children to come home. Like Mughli, American women served as their children's guardian and provided care, protection, and a loving home. Their sons and daughters were some of my students in the U.S. military, now deployed to Afghanistan and Pakistan. Mothers everywhere shared the same maternal instinct to nurture and nourish their families. Mughli was exceptionally courageous as she continued to search for her son. She believed her son to be alive. He disappeared 18 years ago.

Mughli was a single mother. It wasn't her choice. In January 2009, senior journalist Muzamil Jaleel first published a story about Mughli, aptly titled "The pain of a lonely mother" in *Express India*. He told her story:

> "[My son] was born after my husband divorced me. I had no one. I didn't marry again and raised him. He was the only reason for my life. He had never stayed away from home—not even for a single

night. Each day he would return from school and give me a hug. I am still waiting. I wish to hug him once. If they tell me he is dead, I would hug his grave."

Mughli retold the same story in greater detail. "It was a Saturday in the month of September. It was a time of curfew and protests. On the third day, Teli went to school. He was a teacher. He had been teaching at a government school for more than a year. He wasn't a member of a political organization or the militant groups. I would have known if he were involved. There were other days like this, when I heard firing in the distance. It made me nervous and my neighbors gave me tranquilizers to calm me. My feet were numb and I was always anxious when my son stepped outside the house. But that day was different. Teli didn't come home."

Mughli removed her glasses. Her eyes filled with tears. "My eyes have gone blind searching for him. It's been almost 20 years. I have no message from anyone about where he could be. I can't imagine where he is. Every day, I wonder, is he hungry? Is he thirsty? Is he cold? Is he in jail? Is he dead or alive? I just want to know.

When he didn't come home, I ran to the police station. I went to the Army. They said they didn't know where he was. They denied arresting him." During the late 1980s and early 1990s, hundreds of men, young and old, disappeared or were found dead. Decades later, mass graves were uncovered in several districts. The buried were unknown and unmarked.[2] Absent an official investigation, human rights groups reported at least 10,000 men have disappeared since 1990.[3]

She continued. "I didn't sleep that night. I went again and again to the police station. I begged. I pleaded with politicians. I went to the court and filed a petition. The case is ongoing. But nobody knew. I just wanted answers. Once I was so scared I wouldn't leave the house. I began to lose hope when I lost my son. Before he went missing, my father died and then my two sisters passed away. I didn't have a brother."

"My son was everything to me. I sold my jewelry to pay for Teli's education. Now I keep searching and pray he is alive. I can't imagine him dead," Mughli said with a heavy breath.

"My son calls me when I sleep. He is alive in my dreams." Mughli likely accepted her son's death a long time ago, but was still unnerved by not having an official report of his missing body. "I want to know the truth. If he's dead, I want to give him a proper burial," she said, sighing. "I would hug his grave."

Without news of her son, Mughli could not heal. She needed help, perhaps counseling or psychiatric care. A Kashmiri psychiatrist, Dr. Arif Maghribi, sent me a report, "Kashmir in Severe Distress," in which he listed the doctor patient ratio for treating psychiatric diseases is 1:100,00. Many patients are misdiagnosed. Most are given drugs to treat anxiety and depression. As a result of improper care and neglect, Maghribi believed suicide to be a rising trend in Kashmir, especially among women.

This could explain why Mughli tried to take her life by jumping off a bridge. "Strangers stopped me," she said. "Perhaps I am in this world to suffer alone." Like hundreds, if not thousands of women, Mughli was one of Kashmir's silent victims, marked by alienation, helplessness, and a lack of emotional and familial support. Women like Mughli had to find other ways to cope with enduring pain. The real war was not outside her home but in her heart. She desperately tried to find her life's purpose. I suspected she was haunted by self-doubt, wounded by a void created by a son, disappeared, detained or dead. There was nothing more graphic than this.

As I looked around the room, I imagined it once a cozy, lived-in place where mother and son shared conversation and meals together. I imagined Mughli bathing in happiness as her son talked about his students, his school, and how he spent his afternoons off. I imagined her wishing he would choose a bride so she could delight in many grandchildren. I imagined her listening to the caws of myna in her front courtyard as she reclined under the shade of a chinar tree. I imagined her laughing and playing like a child as she aged. But the woman sitting in front of me had a deserted life. She was the abandoned fawn in a rain forest.

With no residual income, Mughli received a monthly pension of seven hundred rupees (eleven U.S. dollars) from the director of her son's school. "Can you live off seven hundred rupees?" she asked. Scanning the room, I could understand why the three-story house she lived in was rundown. She had no money for anything except food and bus fare to the holy place. "Every day, I go to the shrine," she said, with a hopeful smile. "On Fridays, I take a bus to Hazratbal. I pray for my son's return. I thank God for giving me patience."

Holding onto faith helped Mughli fight an unbreakable fortress of sorrow. She nurtured long memories of a boy she raised, without the support of an extended family or nearby neighbors, which was an anomaly in a well-connected society like Kashmir. Here, people upheld honor and noble sacrifice. What more could Mughli do to prove her purity? Being alone was cruel enough.

In the sacred shrine of saints, thousands of worshippers gathered. Men and women bowed in prayer, one for their Prophet, whose strand of hair they believe is sealed like a casket in the mosque; a prayer for the venerated saints they worship like gods; and a prayer for lost loved ones. She believed God listened to blessed men. "God, have mercy," she said, her eyes on the candle burning.

After a long silence, she whispered, "This room will bear me for the rest of my life, just as I thought my son would bear me in my old age. Now I live in his memory." When Jaleel interviewed her, Mughli said, "Even if he is dead, I cannot recognize him after so many years. There would be nothing left of his body." It would seem the lonely mother had accepted her fate. Zahoor and I mourned in silence. Mughli's pain was marked like a tattoo.

If there was ever a woman who deserved to be happy, it was Mughli. I wanted her son to walk through the door. I wanted her to laugh out loud. I wanted neighbors and relatives to visit her. I wanted her to wander through the hills of *Wonderland* triumphantly. I wanted God to find her a husband who cared and a son who stayed with her as she aged. But this dream was hopeless.

We knew it was late. We had to go. At the doorway, Zahoor held her hand, "I will come back. I promise." She had something to look forward to. Zahoor kept his word. I didn't know if I could keep mine. *Would she be alive when I returned?* My inner voice was like the ramblings of a dying man.

Months later, Zahoor told me Mughli passed away. The news of her death came to me like a stripped down sentence.

10

PRISONERS

"We only have our hands to fight with."
--ASIYA ANDRABI, FOUNDER OF WOMEN'S GROUP

"Victims have been randomly picked up, tortured and never even told what they were tortured for."
--UNITED NATIONS REPORT

In every home, there was a story of someone who died, disappeared or was detained. The names of people changed but their wounds and scars were shared. Each family witnessed tragedy or knew someone who did. Even children born after the militant movement had seen excessive use of force. Some lived with guilt for *not* joining the movement. Others hurled rocks and chanted slogans at every opportunity, accepting the risks of imprisonment. In this conflict, women believed it was their duty—even an honor—to contribute to the cause of a free Kashmir. Silence was *not* a virtue.

On the prison floor, the paint on the walls peeled like rain. We sat on the cement floor. An icy wind slipped through the cracked window. Outside, Kashmir turned bridal white. Branches hung heavy with snow. A pallid light reflected off frozen lakes. Blue-green fields looked like sheets of milk. Kashmir would be plagued by another harsh winter.

In Central Jail's waiting room, with the look and stint of a dungeon, I watched Asiya Andrabi fidget in the cold. Cloaked in black, her eyes peered at me through a sliver of cloth. She shifted uncomfortably, her hands clasped between her knees. We had seen each other before. Beneath the thick veil, she had a small round face, dark hair, and pursed lips. I was unprepared for the visit. Within an hour, I could hardly feel my toes.

This was an unlikely encounter. I didn't intend to sneak my way into prison, lying to the prison guards and pretending to be Andrabi's distant relative. Prior to my visit, an Indian scholar Swati Parashar interviewed Andrabi in her home, describing her as a radical religious woman who, as an educated Kashmiri woman, "hardly fits the stereotypical image of a militant."[1] In 1981, Andrabi founded *Dukhtaran-e-Millat* (DeM) to empower women. She demanded seats for women in buses and public transport.[2] She staged protests to protect women from sexual harassment from local authorities, and she held at-home-classes and workshops to train women of their roles and responsibilities in Islam.

Many came to see DeM as a moral police force—the group threatened secular women in public places for their "immoral" appearance and activities. Over time, Andrabi had gained a reputation as a feared female fighter for her attempts to regulate the law, support other conservative groups, and call for an Islamic state. "My strong belief is that all human beings should accept Islam. Only jihad can protect the Islamic faith," she told me, with a slight urgency in her voice.

After everything I had read about her, I still didn't believe Andrabi was capable of imposing a strict, hardline Islam on a valley with diverse customs and creed. In the 1980s, DeM had roughly two hundred members, but in twenty years, membership increased to over five hundred women who believe in Asiya's cause. From the women who adored her, Andrabi was their saving grace.

The prison room had bullet holes in the wall and a small window. In the corner, a bearded man blanketed by a woolen shawl and a white head covering leaned against the dingy wall, his head faced down. At quick glance, I saw a towering figure, tall in size wearing a sesame-colored traditional *salwar kameez*. This man was Asiya's husband, a commander of the *Jamait-ul-Mujahideen* (JuM)—classified by India as a militant group. Asiya told me her husband was arrested for authoring several books on Islam. He was guilty of inciting militants with his writing and therefore, imprisoned for life, of which he served nearly twenty years. Inside prison, her husband completed his Master's and Doctorate in Islamic Studies. Asiya shared her husband's views and believed in a society where only Islam can prevail. When I entered the damp room, the man moved away from his wife to give me space.

Asiya's adopted daughter, Fahmida, was also at my side. She helped me bypass security guards and a barrage of officers with questions about my identity. "Don't speak," she warned me, her hands hidden in black gloves. Through her black veil, she had the dark, illustrious eyes of a panther. She warned me, "The guards will know you're not from here." At the check-in office, where I presented a false name, an Indian guard peered inquisitively at me. He looked at my black boots and a matching velvet dress. "Where are you from?" he asked. "That's not a question you ask a woman," I replied in the way Mama taught me. "I am here to see my aunt."

Fahmida had great admiration for her mother. "She taught me everything about Islam," she said. "Mother used to be my teacher. I am from a village not far from here. My parents were so poor so I came to Mother to learn about religion." She credited Asiya for helping her embrace true Islam. "Before, I was illiterate," the girl said. "Mother showed me how to behave, how to speak, how to protect my honor." Honor in the Islamic world is the opposite of shame. Inside the university classroom, I tell my students "In this part of the world, men view their honor through the actions of their women."

When the girl described honor, I understood it to be a woman's chastity, modesty, and *pardah*, the Urdu word for curtain, or a separation of men and women. In the Islamic world, some mythologized honorable women for being completely covered. In the Western world, the meaning of honor had changed and almost lost its meaning. Scholar James Bowman, author of *Honor: A History*, argued the concept of honor had been discredited, and by the 20th century, the "word doesn't seem to exist anymore."

However, from my experiences as a child in Texas, displays of honor were starkly visible in every-day etiquette of men and women in small towns and rural America. In the Islamic world, honor was deeply attached to the way women dressed. "Through the etiquettes of my Mother, I learned what it meant to be a Muslim," Fahmida said.

Outside the room, Indian security guards manned the black sheet that served as a door. Before entering, the guards stamped visitors' hands with dark blue ink used to take fingerprints. Young men handcuffed, surrounded by guards, walked towards the front gate on their way to the local courthouse for orders of release or indefinite imprisonment. They walked like chained animals.

In Kashmir, Indian authorities had carte blanche power. Passed in 1958, the Armed Forces Special Powers Act (AFSPA) gave Indian authorities "unrestricted and unaccounted powers to carry out operations." Kashmir's then-Chief Minister Omar Abdullah had called for a removal, or revision, of the legislation, and Indian Home Minister P. Chidambaram suggested efforts "to build a consensus within the government to address problems with AFSPA, but no action has been taken."[3] To make matters worse, authorities also invoked the Public Safety Act (PSA), or detention without trial. A Kashmiri held under PSA had no access to a lawyer and no rights to challenge their imprisonment. One critic wrote, prisoners "never receive any compensation for unjust detention and their complaints of torture and ill-treatment are never given any importance."[4]

Asiya's story of life in-and-out of prison is characteristic of power abused by authorities. "I am a threat to the public," she said, dryly. "I am in jail without trial. I don't know when I will be released. If the authorities use the Public Safety Act, I will be locked up for two years. What kind of democracy this is!" On the arctic floor of the prison walls, Asiya bemoaned,

"They say I am a fanatic because I don't believe in secularism. Am I a radical for rejecting the tutelage of the Indian-Hindu government? Am I an extremist for fighting for freedom? I am a Muslim woman who believes in an Islamic state. Under an Islamic rule of law, all people, including religious minorities, will be protected. I stand for humanity, not just for Muslims. It is nonsense to call me anything other than a freedom fighter."

She pointed blame at Kashmir's elected officials for failing to empower women in the way that she hoped: greater political participation; a desegregated society; and an end to Indian occupation and closer ties with Pakistan.

Not everyone agreed or accepted Asiya's vision. To some women, Asiya posed a threat to their secular, liberal ideals. An unnamed Kashmiri woman, now in exile, argued, "She throws acid on women for not wearing the veil. She criticizes women like me for not sharing her beliefs. She's too dangerous." Asiya disagreed. "Our organization never used acid. In fact, I myself test the color [of the water] which we use for splashing, so as to ascertain that it is not harmful," she told Haroon Mirani, a Kashmir-based journalist.[5]

Asiya was a familiar face in the valley. In Arabic, Asiya means nurse and in Swahili, it is comfort. The woman who sat in front of me was like a Rembrandt painting. She had only one feature anyone could visibly see. Her chilling eyes reflected sadness and misery—she might have once seen herself as a victim and made it her life's purpose to fight India. At first, I almost feared Andrabi and expected a menacing woman with a naked sense of terror known for her insect-like eyes and virulent voice.

Despite my initial fear, I felt at ease. Through the cloth that covered her face, I sensed emotional distress. She seemed agitated and unafraid. Perhaps what struck me most was her height. She was barely five feet tall, and yet, this woman caused security forces to panic when she led protests. "The authorities are afraid of me because of the influence I have over women. That's why I am here [in prison]," she said to me in a soft-spoken voice. If I hadn't known of her extreme views, she might have seemed compassionate and comforting.

The first time I heard her name was at a conference at Tufts University near Boston, Massachusetts. I was invited to discuss women in al-Qaeda and share the panel with Parashar, who gave an eye-opening lecture on Kashmir and its women, including the mysterious Andrabi. In a news feature by the British Broadcasting Channel (BBC), Asiya was described as 'a nice militant' who took jihad to Kashmir's women.[6] Other journalists have suggested her name to be synonymous with a terrorist, an Islamic fundamentalist, an al-Qaeda sympathizer, the female version of the Taliban, the leader of a soft terror outfit and much more. "People who don't know me call me a radical because I believe in Islamic law and rights for Muslim women," Asiya later told me.

When we first met in her home, she said, "I believe in jihad. This is a right bestowed on us by Islam." She alluded to the women in Islamic history fourteen hundred years ago who fought valiantly in battle to protect their Prophet. "We are all the same," she said. "We are fighting for what is ours," a reference to the land of Kashmir.

However, freedom wasn't Asiya's main motive. "I created the organization to protect women from rape," she said. Asiya believed women needed protection in a highly militarized, overtly masculine society. Her organization's purpose was to safeguard women from the abuse of authorities.

Rape was a common crime in Kashmir. According to Dr. Arif Maghribi, a psychiatrist who works with rape victims, "rape is an overt act of power, anger, frustration, and aggression than simply a sexual act."[7] An advocate for mental health, Maghribi wrote me a series of emails over a one-year period in which he described the social stigma attached to women who sought counseling for rape.

"In four years, I have seen 24 rape victims," he wrote. Conservative estimates reported 21,000 Kashmiris suffered from mental health problems, "out of which a staggering percentage of patients are females and need constant medication and counseling." A report issued by Human Rights Watch indicated the use of rape "as a means of targeting women whom the security forces accuse of being militant sympathizers; in raping them, the security forces are attempting to punish and humiliate the entire community."[8] Few rapists have been prosecuted and international attention of the crime has been scarce. There are several possibilities for this: the military specifically targets women to dehumanize and disgrace *both* men and women of the valley; the Army exerts its power over the powerless to show they are in control; and rape is a cost of war that is central to many conflicts worldwide.

Since the early 1990s, there have been thousands of rape victims. One estimate claimed over five thousand rape cases committed by security forces were registered between 1989 and 2013.[9] In the fourteen-year period, there were nearly 15,000 cases of molestation by security personnel. By comparison, the same report listed seven cases of rape by militants. In 2012 alone, there were over 300 reported cases registered in Jammu and Kashmir. These figures were indicative of an alarming issue that plagued women and girls, many of whom do not have access to or willingly refuse psychiatric help. They are silent sufferers. Only in rare instances do victims marry.

Maghribi told me of a fourteen-year old girl raped by a close relative, who later married and suffered only minor depression. She may have been the exception—girls who are raped are often isolated in their homes and never marry. In a patriarchal and highly militarized environment, females who experience sexual assault and violence do not come forward. Again, shame is a powerful feeling of humiliation that isolates the victims.

Asiya took great care to protect herself and the women in her group from rape and other abuses. Under her thick ankle-length veil, she pulled out a knife she purchased in Saudi Arabia many years ago. "One of the most important rights we have is to guard our bodies. That is why I train my girls on how to use a knife," she told me.

We first met in her home, which was located in a back alley, invisible to the main road. Her home was like an unused office building with bare essentials, a tiny kitchen and a room with rugs. Asiya placed the falcon-size weapon on the cranberry colored rug. "I am not an extremist. We have only our hands to fight with. We do not carry weapons or use violence," she said, defensively.

I stared at the weapon which looked more like a medieval dagger with its sharp blade enclosed by a crescent-shaped casing. I imagined the weapon could do great damage against its enemy, cutting arms and legs with its narrow, slicing blade resulting in terrible deep wounds. The knife could kill. And so could the sword she hid beneath her veil.

She told me the veil kept her safe. "No one can dare touch me when I dress like this. The Indians say to me 'Asiya, we are more afraid of your *burqa* than we are of the militants,'" she said with a faint smile.

Outside, her two boys were playing. In 1993, when her second son, Ahmad was less than two months, Asiya was arrested for the first time and imprisoned in Jammu jail. According to Asiya, she was charged with promoting pan-Islamic ideals. Mother and son spent the next year in jail together.

"I wasn't given enough food to feed him," she said. "When he was ill, I had to care for him myself. There was no medical care." She recalled the horrid conditions of Jammu prison, infested with lizards, scorpions and snakes. She was lucky he survived. In 1994, Asiya was released. While she and the other female prisoners were not physically abused, the strain of imprisonment "was the worst kind of torture."[10]

Out of prison, Asiya lived like a fugitive, sailing the underground world like a *djinn* or genie. During the next ten years, she avoided an arrest and worked with orphans and widows, whenever possible. She opened rehabilitation centers under her brand, DeM. In 2002, under the guise of the Public Safety Act, Asiya was rearrested and her centers closed. "They [Indians] charged me with running training camps for militants," she said. Without evidence, authorities released her. Three years later, Asiya was back in prison under the same draconian law, charged with forcing girls and women to cover in conservative Islamic dress.

Then, in summer of 2008, the valley escalated into crisis. Protests swept Kashmir against the Indian government for trying to obfuscate land. In an act of solidarity, Asiya joined the collective effort to pressure New Delhi to surrender. As the leader of DeM, Asiya led her own protests, until she was finally arrested and accused of "antinational activities." This would be her third arrest and our second meeting.

"In the beginning of the month, they came to my house to arrest me. The police shelled the house to try to kill me. Windowpanes shattered. When they forced their way in, they beat the women first. My leg began to bleed." She called the press. With local media attention, Asiya barely escaped and went underground for the next nine days. She stormed into the United Nations office and asked officers to observe the protestors and human rights abuses.

"We only have our hands to fight with," she told them. "We have a right to self-determination." She insisted the international body take a stand. Pressure India. Protect protestors. Push for land reform. She wanted the U.N. to do something.

On the Islamic holiday of Eid, authorities arrested the orthodox leader at her house and took her to Udaipur Prison, where she stayed overnight until she moved to Central Jail. This would be the location of our secret meetings.

Before we met, I pictured a fierce woman with intimidating looks —a woman with an outsized reputation for terrifying the Indian Army. *Can one woman strong-arm the authorities with her conservative beliefs? Was she really that frightening? Was this woman's goal to tyrannize the Army, as they had claimed? Or was she simply one woman committed to change? Perhaps her only crime was the sword underneath her black dress. If I had felt threatened, I might have carried a weapon, too.*

In the arctic prison room, Asiya complained of every-day conditions. "I never see the sun. I'm locked inside for 12 hours a day. The cell is dirty. It stinks. The mice are the size of cats. I have chronic neck pain. I can't sleep. I sit in one place with a thin blanket. The cold will kill me," she said, rubbing her hands together. I sensed her mind flooded with anguished adjectives or hysterics lost in translation. A landslide of emotions whirled like a tornado. "I read the holy book and pray. That's all I can do," she moaned. From the high window, the cottony blue sky and distant clouds drifted like faraway balloons and was thrilling to watch.

In that moment, I was numbed by the cold and the pain in the woman's eyes. I sensed her deep frustration for being misjudged and misplaced as a terrorist when she believed she had a right to protect her gender. *Is it legal here to chain a woman for improving the lives of women? Asiya is an educator, teacher, and lecturer on Islam, even if it is her own version of the faith. Could the Army bully this woman for hosting women's workshops? Could the military shackle a woman for her spirituality?*

Asiya stared at the ground, her gloved hands at the back of her neck. She looked miserable as descending cold air crept through her, like spasmodic lightning. She groaned of high cholesterol, blood pressure, and the chills. I didn't know how Asiya made it through bone-chilling nights.

Next to me, her daughter Fahmida, who seemed untouched by winter, said blankly, "Mother was taken to a hospital when she collapsed with fever. She was shivering uncontrollably. They did a quick check-up and brought her back to prison." Asiya grew more agitated. "I can't stay in the hospital for one night. It does not matter how sick I am. I am brought back to prison the same day," she said, angrily. Later that year, when she was released, Asiya began a slow recovery and continued to lead protests and meetings for members of DeM. There, she stood strong.

In 2010, security personnel invoked the PSA to arrest Asiya again for supposedly indoctrinating Kashmiri women. She was dubbed the dangerous ideologue. Authorities advertently moved her from one prison to another. "They wanted to discourage me and tried to break my will, but I am a pious believer. All I want to do is serve my religion which is not possible under Indian supremacy," she said. After her release, Asiya returned home, almost broken.

My guide and friend, Samie, sent me an update. "In her condition, she can't afford to continue her work. As I observed, she can't sit properly because of a severe back pain. She can't talk or breathe easily due to bronchitis. She has high blood pressure and osteoarthritis. She is currently under [medical] treatment. For the time being, she is discreet about her work." Keeping a low profile was in Asiya's best interests. It was the only way out of prison.

The Army tried to paralyze women like Asiya. And yet, she continued to practice her faith and worked tirelessly on educating local women on their rights. Hers was a way of life under threat. *She is undamaged*, I thought. *She is determined, perhaps destined, to continue fighting for women, even if it will cost her own life. And while I may not have always agreed with her politics and her traditional views, I had to applaud her promise to the women she served—she would never abandon them.*

Wounded by prison, Asiya lived in an uncertain present. She worried endlessly about another possible arrest. Her greatest anxiety was her children. She sent her eldest to live with her sister in Malaysia when he was nineteen, and her youngest (then a teenager) stayed with her.

With a husband in prison, one son sent away for his safety, and a boy by her side, Asiya's life had been destroyed. The only person *not* in prison was her adopted daughter. Her eyes swelled. "It is very tough to live and manage without a husband," she bemoaned, "I am unable to provide for my children when I am in jail or hiding."

We said good-bye in muffled voices. I looked back at her home in a maze of alleys and headed to the main road. The winter sun was blotting into the mountains. I walked away thinking of Asiya and women like her, uncompromising in their cause, even while trying to care for their families. I often wondered about Asiya's children: how boys grew up without a mother; or a daughter touched by the suffering of her mother. I had no words to express my own grief at the thought of her children separated from their mother.

For years, Asiya's shadow chased me as I thought about her ultra-conservative values and the choices she made to uphold them. I wondered if Asiya's love for her land and Kashmiri women crippled her. *Would she regret her decisions?* "In spite of all her sufferings, Asiya is dedicated to her cause," Samie told me. I had no doubt Asiya is determined to bring orthodox Islam to Kashmir.

That night, I dreamt of the prison and the two boys in gray sweaters handcuffed, leaving Central Jail, with their heads lowered and guarded by prison attendants. I had no way of knowing who they were, only that they belonged to a family. I could only imagine their mothers crying for their release.

CONCLUSION
LOCKDOWN

"India has pushed us into the Stone Age."
--LOCAL KASHMIRI

"Silence is the loudest sound."
--ARUNDHATI ROY, INDIAN AUTHOR & ACTIVIST

On August 5, 2019, Kashmir went dark. The Indian State banned phone and Internet service indefinitely. Kashmir was subjected to a new form of cruelty. India forced an entire population into debilitating silence—a mental, physical, social and psychological lockdown. Although lockdowns were common in Kashmir, the extent of this silence was unprecedented.

A week before the communications blackout, India's Prime Minister Narendra Modi, who won his election by encouraging anti-Muslim bigotry, flooded Kashmir with thousands of troops, detained hundreds of prominent Muslims, and asked foreign tourists to leave the valley.[1] Kashmiris had no clue of what was about to happen.

And so, without warning on that summer morning, the Indian State revoked Articles 370 and 35A of the Indian Constitution that had protected Kashmir's special status as a Muslim-majority state. The article granted Kashmiris some autonomy and special privileges as a people, such as the right to buy and own their land. The Permanent Residents Law or Article 35A prevented outsiders from owning property or landing a state job in Kashmir. Under the article, decisions on foreign affairs, defense, and communications remained under the jurisdiction of Kashmir's central government. That changed on August 5th when the Indian State declared that the fundamental rights of Kashmiris no longer mattered.

Kashmir was forever changed.

So why now? Some claim that Modi and the supra-Hindu nationalist Bharatiya Janata Party (BJP) had long opposed Article 370; that the Indian PM had promised the article's dismissal in his 2019 election manifesto; that Modi and his party-supporters had long intended to integrate Kashmir into the rest of the country; and that the PM believed he could bring economic growth to the valley and long-lasting peace. Perhaps India's move was designed to change the demographics of the valley and threaten the very identity, interests, and integrity of Kashmir. In a *New York Times* op-ed, "Silence Is the Loudest Sound," famed Indian activist Arundhati Roy wrote:

> "[India] turned all of Kashmir into a giant prison camp. Seven million Kashmiris were barricaded in their homes, Internet connections were cut and their phones went dead...For Kashmiris, this has been an old, primal fear."[2]

The dismissal of Article 370 forced Kashmiris to abide by the Indian Constitution. Kashmiris were thus required to comply with all Indian laws much like the people of other states, while non-Kashmiris were given the right to buy land in the pristine valley—a move that Hindu right-wing groups welcomed with joy. Indian leaders publicly promised development to the region and justified their actions in the name of *democracy*, an artificial word to Kashmiris who have been tortured and traumatized by India and its false promise for decades.

India's decision to implement a policy of forced isolation is arguably the worst form of control and coercion. For months on end, the communications blackout destroyed the way of life in Kashmir. Famous Kashmiri graphic novelist Malik Sajad paints a vivid and dark picture of life in Kashmir with the apt title, *We Have Been in a Lockdown for Three Decades*. Through cartoons, Sajad illustrates the way Kashmiris have suffered through lockdown since 1990. *It is a life not lived as India imposes curfews and uses brute force to control an unarmed population.*

Since August 2019, the communications ban imprisoned Kashmiris inside their own homes. They could not call their neighbors, friends, and other family members living in the valley, much less those outside of Kashmir. Without access to loved ones or the news, a silence of uncertainty permeated the valley. Feelings of resentment, rage, defeat, and doubt against the Indian State were amplified. The blackout reaffirmed to Kashmiris that India's efforts would remain insincere and incapable of seeking a peaceful, political solution to the decades-long conflict.

In the West, or anywhere else, a life without the Internet is unthinkable, if not unimaginable. The entire global economy would collapse. Media would cease to exist. The foundation for human rights and democracy valued in the West would disintegrate. The long-term impact of a communications ban would create anxiety, alarm, and agitation for those used to living with access to a free and fair communications system. The loss of the Internet on any society would cripple, if not crumble, global interconnectedness that is vital to our everyday existence.

In Kashmir, losing contact with the outside world and others across the valley was destabilizing, disorienting and dehumanizing. Which is why the blackout in Kashmir should have been declared a human rights violation. The blackout should have been considered illegal, but because it is *not* illegal, India continued to suppress Kashmiris with a communications ban—an arbitrary and autocratic move. Most recently, in late June 2020, the Army's battle with militants was followed by a three-day shutdown; there was no phone and Internet service in southern Kashmir. The echo of silence was inexpressible. During the communications blackout, I lost contact with the people I love the most in Kashmir--they are my second family.

A week before the blackout, my best friend sensed something. "More soldiers are being sent here every day. I have a terrible feeling about what is about to happen," he told me via WhatsApp, the social media platform many Kashmiris depend on for communication. As usual, I dismissed the warning. *This can't happen again*, I thought. *I remembered the time of the floods when I lost touch with my friend for eight days. Then, I had feared the worst. The most dangerous thoughts enter the mind when plagued by fear, the venom of distraction. It was a feeling I desperately wanted to avoid.* I asked if there had been a local "encounter," a reference to a terrorist attack or clashes between militants and the Indian Army, which justified the security forces' increased security tactics and house raids.

"What do you hear?" I asked, waiting for the sound of jets flying overhead or tanks rolling into his village.

"Nothing," he said.

"Then nothing will happen to you or anyone else," I reassured him. I could not have predicted the Indian State's impending action, driven by antipathy and aggression against the Kashmiri people. It was a move that would shatter—albeit temporarily—the people's collective aspiration for justice, freedom and hope for Kashmir. No one could have anticipated the horrors to come.

On August 5th, my friend's phone went dead. The silence stretched on. One day. Two days. Three days turned into 20 days. India inflicted the pain of silence on thousands of Kashmiris. Stripped of communication, Kashmiris experienced silence as a new form of warfare. The international community turned to the United Nations to oppose India's actions, but nothing changed. Watching the news, my heart began to break. *A pained heart can be compared to brain death, which is why we must hear the sound of a loved one's voice to feel alive and whole again. That sound is a steady clarion of safety, and without it, the rhythmic warmth of life slips away.*

I was not alone. Thousands of Kashmiris living inside the valley were hopelessly dialing their dead phones, expecting a signal, trying to contact friends and families around the world. People were forced to use primitive communication methods, passing hand-written notes or sending word-of-mouth messages. An ambulance driver told the DW online news: "If they [India] were planning to starve people to death like this, why did not they just kill all the people here and grab the land?"[3]

All across the valley, Kashmiris suffered unspeakable silence. Kashmiri students in New Delhi and other Indian states were frantically trying to reach their parents. A Kashmiri girl, who I will call Daisy, tried endlessly to contact her parents from New Delhi, where she was studying. My American friend and her husband in Washington, D.C. were contacting anyone they knew to reach his parents in Srinagar city. Nights of dread and days of anguish for not being able to reach their families created infinite contempt for the Indian State. All anyone wanted was a comforting voice, a recognizable sound to drown out emotional panic.

The horrors of *not* knowing if a loved one is safe or unsafe, sick or healthy, at home or in jail, is a dreadful way to live. The silence in Kashmir was another symptom of the devastation of war, a sign for hurting survivors, and a reminder to those of us who cared deeply for the Kashmiris that occupation will eventually lead to more violence, vehemence, and bloodshed. I have been following the events in Kashmir for over a decade, and so little has changed.

In desperation, I found someone who passed me the working number of a local police station in the valley. The police are different from the Indian Army—the police are comprised of local Kashmiris and the Army is made of non-Kashmiris. At this point, only the police offered to help search for my friend.

A mature voice answered. I had one chance to convince the police officer that I needed to send a message to my friend. *What would I say first? How would I say it? Why should the officer help me?* I thought. *I wanted to believe my friend was at home, safe with his family. Maybe he's sleeping or walking through his apple orchard. Even so, I knew he would be crippled with worry, knowing that we have never been apart like this, except during the natural disaster. That was a different time. This is a state-imposed blackout that was too animalistic and crude, a deafness that jackhammered my senses.*

I was prepared. I had written down all possible questions and answers on a notepad. I would have to explain why an American woman needed to know the whereabouts of a local Kashmiri. *Is concern for a dear friend enough?* Whatever I must have said, the officer understood. He sympathized. I could only imagine the countless other calls he received with similar requests to find their loved ones.

"Call tomorrow at this time and he will be here," he assured me. For a single moment, I was uplifted and could calm the landscape of emotions that triggered the obsession of waiting for someone in a distant land. That night, I slept peacefully.

When I called again, the officer answered and handed the phone to the friend I had been waiting for. The officer found his home and had delivered a message. He told my friend to come to the station the next day at 4:00 pm. He arrived early, eagerly sitting near the phone. We had less than two minutes.

"You found me," he exclaimed with relief. "I tried leaving home three times to find a place with phone service. Each time, the roads were blocked. Finally, I made it to Jammu during the night (an eight-hour drive) and there was still no service. I had to come back home." I sensed the strong, regular heart rhythm of a Kashmiri I had grown to admire.

In a hushed tone, he told me to be patient another week or so. He would travel to New Delhi, India's capital city, so he could have uninterrupted phone and Internet service. There, he would contact me and other loved ones who were worried for his safety. All I had to do was wait. One day. Two days. Three days…I lost count of time.

And so, after 20 days of anticipation, I had the comfort of knowing my friend was safe. I felt myself again. The weight of waiting and timelessness ended and the sickening knot in my stomach went away. It thrilled me to know he and his family were safe and healthy at home. He survived the prolonged silence with enduring patience, as had so many Kashmiris, for they had the gift of forbearance.

A month later, in September 2019, thousands of Kashmiris were arrested. They were beaten and tortured on false charges, a typical Indian ploy to dehumanize a population. *Al Jazeera* reported the stories of local men and women who had suffered from electric shocks and electrocutions. "I was beaten with sticks, rifle butts and they kept asking me why I went for a protest march. I kept telling them I didn't, but they didn't stop. After I fainted, they used electric shocks to revive me," said a 22-year old torture-survivor.[4]

As the torture continued, the international community issued statements to the United Nations and warned against the long-time consequences of state-imposed isolation. The crisis put Kashmir on the map for many Westerners unfamiliar with the conflict. Despite the gestures and calls for peace, India refused to change its policy. The cry for reason must have seemed like a loose net of words to Indian PM Modi, whose decision to continue the blackout for months was also contested within the Indian Parliament by opposition leaders. They feared the worst outcome when a country subdues a people—the epic tragedy of Kashmir *is* India's national story.

In September, my friend finally called from New Delhi. He told me about his harrowing escape out of the village, traveling through Srinagar by night and through the mountains of Jammu, followed by a long train ride to India's capital city. His total travel time was 20 hours. Despite his exhaustion, he had the energy of a boy reunited with freedom after weeks of lockdown. We talked effortlessly without the surge of silence that had kept us in the dark. When he finally returned home to Kashmir, we lived with the absence of each other's words until the Internet was restored.

By mid-December 2019, Kashmiris had been without the Internet and cell phone service for 134 days, the longest ban of its kind enforced by a democratic country. Many expressed outrage and criticized India's policies in Kashmir, including Indian-American

Congresswoman Pramila Jayapal, a Democrat from Washington, D.C., and the first Indian American woman ever elected to the U.S. House of Representatives.

In early December, Jayapal introduced a Congressional resolution with U.S. Representative Steve Watkins from Kansas to urge India to lift the restrictions on communications in Kashmir as swiftly as possible. The resolution insisted India "preserve religious freedom for all and end [the] communications blockade and mass detentions in Jammu & Kashmir."[5] Watkins called on India to "uphold democratic values" and expressed concern with New Delhi's continued human rights violations. Addressing the U.S. Congress, Watkins said:

> "Madam Speaker, today I rise in support of democracy and freedom for the people of Jammu and Kashmir and the importance of protecting religious minorities in the region...Since the Indian government rescinded Article 370 of their Constitution, there have been curfews, and some 4,000 people have been detained, which includes children as young as nine years old...this situation cannot stand."[6]

Two days after introducing the resolution, six more American lawmakers joined as co-sponsors. Jaypal's effort to raise awareness on the Kashmir issue in the U.S. government and pressure exerted on India from other Western countries, including attempts from foreign diplomat to visit the region (which were suspiciously denied), likely compelled the Indian State to take limited action.

Seven months later, in March 2020, India partially lifted the official ban on blacklisted websites, some social media platforms, mobile (2G only), and fixed-line Internet services. It is arbitrary to express the arrangement of words, emotions, and thoughts that pulsated through Kashmir. While people were elated to periodically communicate again (as communications restrictions continued periodically), their suffering could not easily be dismissed. That they had survived the blackout without resorting to violence or civil unrest was a testimony to their timeless tolerance. The caravan of cries and calls for frantic indignation would later come from militants, whose endless battle for freedom through violent action would remain undeterred. So long as India imposed its will with arrogance against an entire population, the militants' wrath would be unchanged.

Today, Kashmir is *the* most militarized zone in the world. In 70-plus years, more than 100,000 people, mostly civilians, have been killed in the conflict by Indian forces. According to Roy, "thousands have 'disappeared,' and tens of thousands have passed through torture chambers that dot the valley like a network of small-scale Abu Ghraibs," a reference to former U.S. military prison camps in Iraq.

For years, India has used illegal weapons to "contain" Kashmiris, especially its children. This includes pellet-firing shotguns used against protestors throwing stones and shouting slogans of freedom. As a result, India has blinded hundreds of Kashmiris, including children and teenagers who were shot during the unrest in 2010 and 2016. Human rights organizations, healthcare professionals, and activists have warned of the deep physical and psychological trauma from the pellet guns, but the police argue that it is the "least lethal" option for crowd-control.

More recently, India has forced another lockdown on Kashmir. Since March 2020, due to the COVID-19 pandemic, the Indian State has mandated all Kashmiris stay inside their homes to contain the spread of the virus. This is the only lockdown that makes sense as other worldwide countries have also imposed stay-at-home orders. As of this writing, the virus has claimed hundreds of lives.

Despite the number of deaths, the stay-at-home order has created a more serious health crisis. Kashmiris in need of medical care for other illnesses are barred from leaving their homes, and thus, they suffer silently without medication and the help they deserve. In some villages, doctors and other medical staff are nearly impossible to reach. Worse, human rights organizations have expressed concern that the Indian State will use the pandemic outbreak to further restrict Kashmir's civil liberties and change the demographics of the valley.

In April 2020, India changed its decades-old Domicile Law and offered new protections to non-Kashmiris. The law grants domicile status to anyone who has stayed in the region for 15 years—this gives legal permission to non-Kashmiris to gain permanent residence in the valley. Under the new law, domiciles, which include 700,000 migrant workers, can qualify for resettlement and greater job opportunities.

Muslims fear the new law will change the demographics of Kashmir.[7] The Kashmiri Muslim-majority population (over 70%) are concerned the new law will allow *other* minorities (namely, Hindus) to settle in the valley; over time, Muslims will become a minority in their own homeland. A prominent Kashmiri journalist, Riyaz Wani, called India's move to open Jammu and Kashmir for outside settlement "another Palestine in the making."[8]

The law's greatest support comes from India's far-right Hindu party, which has used indiscriminate violence against Kashmiri Muslims to marginalize them. A Srinagar-based political commentator, Gowhar Geelani, posted on Facebook: "Even during a pandemic of colossal magnitude, a party is going ahead with its Hindutva project [a political movement and ideology advocating a Hindu state and way of life] to further dispossess Kashmir politically, economically and psychologically." It is clear that the Domicile Law is designed to change the Kashmir Valley into a Hindu state and further suppress the rights of its Muslim residents.

In neighboring Pakistan, Pakistani Prime Minister Imran Khan charged India with violating international law. Pakistani scholars, journalists, politicians and writers hold regular talks on the Kashmir crisis. For example, on May 15, 2020, The University of Lahore held a webinar titled "Kashmiris in the Age of Detention: What Changes for the Kashmiris Pre and Post-Pandemic?" to explore the current medical crisis. Former Pakistan Ambassador to the U.S., Dr. Maleeha Lodhi, stated that Kashmiris are particularly vulnerable to COVID-19. "India has denied Kashmiris medical supplies...journalists reporting on the conflict have been arrested; political leaders have been detained and multiple lines of communication shut down," she said.

Pakistani professor Awais Raoof emphasized the ongoing human rights abuses by Indian security forces only encourages radicalization.

Outside the region, on July 4, 2020, British Kashmiris in the United Kingdom gathered in a virtual conference titled "Twin Lockdowns in Kashmir" to highlight the suffering of innocent Kashmiris. They called on the British government to pressure India to allow U.K. charities inside Kashmir to help those who needed food and medicine.

Earlier this year, in the United States, American-Kashmiri activists and supporters of the Kashmiri people held protests in the nation's capital of Washington, D.C. and across New York City to call attention to the ongoing conflict. On February 3, 2020, Kashmir Solidarity Day was held in New York to address India's unlawful annexation of Kashmir and the Kashmiri people's right to self-determination. An American spokesman and Secretary General of the World Kashmir Awareness Forum, Dr. Ghulam Nabi Fai, stated: "Kashmir continues to bleed...A deliberate, systematic and officially sanctioned massive campaign of brutal oppression against the people of Kashmir is still on the increase." At the event, a young human rights activist, Fatima Khan, said: "we need to be the voice of the voiceless." Participants of the event urged the United Nations and the international community to stop India's illegitimate moves in Kashmir.

Days later, on February 16, 2020, the United Nations Secretary-General declared, "We have taken a position that UN resolutions (on Kashmir) should be implemented; there should be ceasefire and human rights should be respected." These discussions and debates are vital to raising awareness of the Kashmir conflict. The hope is that a collective global effort can exert some pressure on the Indian State to recognize the Kashmiris' desire for peace. The growing interest on Kashmir by human rights activists, scholars, writers, peace builders, and policymakers is a positive sign that the conversation for peace will continue for as long as it is necessary to resist Indian occupation.

For now, India remains in control of the valley. The conflict has had a negative impact on the lives of Kashmiri women and girls. Many have been widowed, raped, jailed, tortured—their sons, husbands, brothers, uncles, cousins, and fathers have been killed. The ongoing turmoil has crippled the lives of these women with curfews that last months and other excessive human rights violations, most of which are unchecked.

Today, the lockdown and unreliable access to communication has stifled the way of life for most Kashmiris. As of this writing, streets are empty—except for a few local cars—and crowds of protestors are non-existent. Schools and universities are closed. Markets and neighborhood medical stores open for a short period of time. The Army patrols with rifles tugged at their shoulders in the landscape of ruination.

Despite the hardship, Kashmiri women will *not* be silenced forever. The current lockdown will fail to quiet a people with unlimited talent and tenacity. When restrictions are lifted, women will march again and continue to make calls to the United Nations to mediate the international conflict. Women believe there *is* a solution to this intractable dispute. It is my hope that the international community will support these women and pressure India to end militarization.

If we continue to side with India, and ignore the rights of Kashmiris, then we become passive participants of their tragedy. We must be the voice for Kashmir's voiceless. As an American, and a human rights defender, it is imperative we collectively support their path to peace.

THANK YOU FOR READING

If you enjoyed this book, please leave a review on Amazon. Reviews are important and greatly appreciated.

Just to say thanks for reading my book, I would like to give you a FREE Unpublished Chapter! Click on the link below.

DOWNLOAD THE FREE CHAPTER

Join the newsletter for book updates, free gifts, and analysis you won't get anywhere else.

https://farhanaqazi.com/

A CALL TO ACTION

Over the years, so many people have asked me: what can I do to help? How can I support the Kashmiri people? The first step is awareness. Please share these stories on social media to build understanding and make the world aware of the conflict's ongoing impact on the lives of women (and men). To stay current on news in Kashmir, you can follow: The Greater Kashmir, The Kashmir Observer, Kashmir-BBC News, and Kashmir-The New York Times.

Another vital step is empowering local women. I support local village women in Indian-held Kashmir to improve their lives. These women weave shawls from their homes and neighborhood co-ops to support their families. Your purchase of this book will help the women of Kashmir. Thank you for caring.

Join the newsletter for insightful analysis you won't find anywhere else. Visit www.farhanaqazi.com

ACKNOWLEDGMENTS

I am profoundly grateful to the people of Kashmir who welcomed me into their homes and trusted me with their stories. My guides gifted me with their insight and protection—I am eternally grateful.

To adventurist Robert Young Pelton, who dared me to go to Kashmir. To Dr. Eric Selbin, Dr. Jerrold Post, Sherra Babcock, Dr. Hassan Abbas, Dr. Akbar Ahmed, Dr. Robert Snyder, Danielle Khan, Naureen Safdar Butt, Heidi Panetta, Melissa Arciero-Durr, Tanisha Tingle, Betsy Ashton, Dr. Suzanne Chamier, Audra Grant, Abigail Esman, Judit Maul, Anastasia Colombo, Chris Carr, and my kind-hearted students at The George Washington University for believing in me.

The third edition benefited greatly from my beta readers, who provided useful feedback. Thank you for your time and support. A special thanks to Isabel and Danielle for your editorial eye and my special assistant, Deisha, for helping me reach readers in more ways than one.

My family is my lifeline. To my late maternal grandmother, Imtiaz Mir, for her love of Kashmir; my late paternal grandfather, Rahimutallah Qazi, a Sergeant in the British Army; and my parents for the gift of education. Finally, I am indebted to my best friend. Without him, this book would not have been written.

ABOUT THE AUTHOR

Farhana Qazi is an award-winning speaker and scholar on conflicts in Muslim world. Born in northern Pakistan and raised in Texas, she straddles the East and West and brings multiple perspectives to her work.

As a young analyst, she began her study of conflict in the US government, where she briefed senior policy makers and practitioners. Upon leaving government service, she continued her work as a researcher and traveled to Muslim countries to understand the origins of conflict. She is the founder of Global Insights, LLC, where she conducts independent research, provides training on Islam and conflicts in the Muslim world, and works with clients to resolve complex problems in conflict-prone countries.

As an Adjunct Professor at The George Washington University, Farhana teaches Gender, Conflict & Security and Women in Violent Extremism. Inside the classroom, she addresses the impact of war and prolonged conflict on women. She examines the different roles and contributions made by women in war.

As a senior instructor for the US military, she trained hundreds of men and women in uniform on Islam, Pakistan, the Middle East, and global threats. She has trained officers all across America and foreign liaison officers (military and police) from Saudi Arabia, Bahrain, Kuwait, South Korea, and Pakistan, to name a few.

Farhana is a recipient of the 21st Century Leader Award, presented by the National Committee on American Foreign Policy in New York, for her training and service to the US military, and she received the Distinguished Humanitarian Award from Southwestern

University, her alma mater in Texas, for her research on women in war.

As an expert, Farhana has appeared in mainstream media: CNN, the BBC, PBS, National Public Radio, Fox News, C-Span, Bloomberg, ABC News, MSNBC, Canadian national television, Voice of America, Al Jazeera, and more. She is a graduate of the National Security Studies Program at the George Washington University and holds a Bachelor of Arts with a major in Political Science and a minor in French from Southwestern University in Georgetown, Texas.

Farhana lives in Virginia. She loves the outdoors: walking along placid blue waters; hiking dry mountains; and spending time in Langkawi. To learn more about her research, visit www.farhanaqazi.com

 facebook.com/farhanaqaziauthor

 twitter.com/farhanaqazi

 instagram.com/farhanaqaziwriter

 linkedin.com/in/farhanaqazi

READING GROUP GUIDE

SECRETS OF THE KASHMIR VALLEY

by

FARHANA QAZI

Questions and topics for discussion

1. Farhana Qazi explores the origins of the Kashmir conflict. What events created the conflict?

1. Has the conflict affected women differently?

1. What roles have women played in this conflict? How do their roles differ from men?

1. How would you define a gendered war?

1. Why is sexual-based violence a weapon of choice for male security forces?

1. What are the benefits of protests? Are their disadvantages to the protest movement?

1. What were some of the most surprising or interesting facts that you learned from this book?

1. Who are the most visible women of Kashmir?

1. Discuss the international community's role in bringing peace to Kashmir.

1. What is the most striking image, phrase, or scene from the book?

NOTES

1. Mama's War

1. Wolpert, Stanley, *Jinnah of Pakistan*, (Oxford University: UK), 1984
2. "Jinnah and women's emancipation," *Dawn*, December 22-28, 2005, p. 6

2. Remembrance

1. According to British author and historian, Victoria Schofield, "what Radcliffe did was conform to the suggested boundaries [that had] already been worked out in February 1964 before the [British] Cabinet Mission arrived in India." Email correspondence in February 2015.
2. Borrowed from Kashmiri-America poet, Shahid Ali, who wrote a verse of poetry titled *The Country Without a Post Office.*
3. From *Cracking India* by Bapsi Sidwa
4. Feng, Pin-chia, "Birth of Nations: Representing the Partition of India in Bapsi Sidhwa's *Cracking India*," in Chang Gung Journal of Humanities and Social Sciences, 4:2 (October 2011), 225-240
5. Email correspondence in February 2015 with Victoria Schofield, who is an author of several books on India and Pakistan.
6. Butalia, Urvashi, *The Other Side of Silence,* (Durham, N.C.: Duke University Press), 2000
7. Bharadwaj, Prashant; Asim Khwaja and Atif Mian, "The Big March: Migratory Flows after the Partition of India," in *Economic and Political Weekly*, Harvard University, August 30, 2008, p. 40.
8. Ibid., p. 39
9. Butalia, excerpt from her book
10. *A Natural History of the Senses* by Diane Ackerman, p. 117

3. Militarization

1. Arundhati Roy interview with Democracy Now, October 2010
2. Roy, Arundhati, "Azadi, The Only Thing Kashmiris Want," in *Kashmir: The Case for Freedom*, (Verso, London) 2011
3. Manasa Mohan, "Kashmir ki Kali turned eyesore to draw attention to pellet injuries in Valley," *Hindustan Times*, August 9, 2016. Accessed at: https://www.hindustantimes.com/india-news/kashmir-ki-kali-turned-eyesore-to-draw-attention-to-pellet-injuries-in-valley/story-ctTURqlhiZ7rpDzHo-NEUKP.html

4. Zubair Lone and Gowhar Hassan, "Kashmir's Forgotten Culture of Cinema Theaters," March 14, 2018, *The Quint.*

5. Ibid.

6. Sheikh Qayoom, "Srinagar likely to get its first multiplex cinema theatre," *India Narrative,* June 21, 2020. Accessed at: https://indianarrative.com/india/srinagar-likely-to-get-its-first-multiplex-cinema-theatre-3498.html

7. Rushdie, Salman, *Shalimar The Clown,* (Random House, 2006)

8. A detailed timeline of events can be accessed at PBS Frontline, http://www.pbs.org/wgbh/pages/frontline/shows/ira/etc/cron.html

9. Frady, Marshall, *Martin Luther King, Jr.* (Penguin, 2002) p. 124

10. For a firsthand account of the Maoist rebels, see Roy, Arundhati, *Walking with the Comrades,* (Penguin, 2011).

11. Ibid., p.123

12. Ibid.

4. Bomb Girl

1. For an accurate list of the Prophet's wives and notable women, see *Great Women of Islam* by Mahmood Ahmad Dhadanfar (2001)

2. Busool, Assad Nimer, *Muslim Women Warriors,* (Al-Huda, Chicago), p. 35

3. Heath, Jennifer, *The Scimitar and the Veil,* (Hidden Spring, NJ), 2004, p. 215

4. Qazi, Farhana, "The *Mujahidaat*" in *Women, Gender and Terrorism* (editor, Laura Sjoberg), University of Georgia Press, 2011, p. 30

5. Bloom, Mia, *Bombshell,* (Univ of Penn Press, 2011)

6. Article was published under my former name, Farhana Ali. Co-authored with Dr. Jerold Post, "The History and Evolution of Martyrdom in the Service of Defensive Jihad: An Analysis of Suicide Bombers in Current Conflicts," *Social Science Research Journal,* Vol. 75, No. 2, Summer 2008, pp. 619-620.

7. Stern, Jessica, *Terror in the Name of God,"* (Harper Collins: New York), 2003

8. Burke, S.M. and Quraishi, Salim al-Din, *British Raj in India,* (Oxford University Press, New York), 1995, p. 28

9. Ibid, p. 35

10. Chakrabarty, Manas and Agarwala, Vidyawati (eds), *Women and Politics in India,* (Associated Publishers, Ambala), 2006

11. Statement made by human rights activist Rita Manchanda.

5. Female Fighters

1. To learn more about gendered nationalism in Kashmir, see *Resisting Occupation,* edited by Haley Duschinski, Mona Bhan, Ather Zia, and Cynthia Mahmood, (Univ. of Penn. Press, PA), 2018, pp. 24-28.

2. Fabian Hartwell, "Burhan Wani and the Masculinities of the State," *Journal of Extreme Anthropology,* Vol. 1, No. 3, p. 127.

3. The op-ed was published under my former name, Farhana Ali. Article can be accessed online, http://articles.baltimoresun.com/2005-12-13/news/0512130414_1_-suicide-female-attacks

4. "Asifa Bano Story," *Stars unfolded*. For detailed information, see https://starsun-folded.com/asifa-bano-kathua-rape-victim/ and https://starsunfolded.com/asifa-bano-story/

5. "Six men convicted in the rape and murder of 8-year old girl that shocked India," *Washington Post*, June 10, 2019. Accessed at: https://www.washingtonpost.-com/world/asia_pacific/six-men-convicted-in-rape-of-8-year-old-girl-that-shocked-india/2019/06/10/cde7b17c-8b5f-11e9-b162-8f6f41ec3c04_story.html. Also see, "All about Criminal Law Bill 2018 on child rape passed in Lok Sabha," *India Today*, July 31, 2019. Accessed at: https://www.indiatoday.in/india/story/child-rape-criminal-law-amendment-bill-2018-1301038-2018-07-31

6. Ackerman, p. 245

6. Protestors

1. Accessed online, http://www.opendemocracy.net/5050/ruth-rosen/women-and-language-of-peace-protest

2. Waheed, Ch.1

3. Khan, Shahnawaz, "Bitta Karate distances from controversial interview," *Kashmir Newz*, Nov. 3, 2006, accessed at www.kashmirnewz.com/n00052.html

7. Political Activist

1. "Delhi's Abu Garib," article given to me by Anjum, the author

2. Starr, Douglas, "The Interview," *The New Yorker*, December 9, 2013, p. 42

3. Samie Shah gave me a two-page handwritten document listing the early martyrs or freedom fighters of Kashmir in 1931 across the valley in different districts and in Srinagar city.

4. Interview accessed at http://thealternative.in/inclusivity/through-the-eyes-of-prisoner-100/

5. Habib's book, p. 139

6. "Kashmiri Women Activist, Prisoner #100 Speaks" by Mushtaq ul-Haq Ahmad Sikander

7. Anjum gave me a bound notebook with several articles, including this one she wrote in May 2008 for *Honor*, a local Kashmiri publication, titled "Delhi's Abu Garib."

8. "Kashmiri Women Activist, Prisoner #100 Speaks" by Mushtaq ul-Haq Ahmad Sikander

8. Mothers of Martyrs

1. "Afzal Guru made us proud: Maqbool Butt's mother," Kashmir Media Service. Accessed at: http://www.kmsnews.org/news/2013/02/10/afzal-guru-made-us-proud-maqbool-butt's-mother.html

2. Jeffrey Gettleman, "In Kashmir, Blood and Grief in an Intimate War: 'These Bodies Are Our Assets," *The New York Times*, August 1, 2018.

3. Fahad Shah, "Kashmir's Young Rebels," *The Diplomat*, August 22, 2015, accessed at: https://thediplomat.com/2015/08/kashmirs-young-rebels/

4. Aasif Sultan, "Did Burhan pick up a gun after his brother was killed? *Kashmir Narrator*, October 14, 2017. Accessed at: http://kashmirnarrator.com/fact-check-burhan-pick-gun-brother-killed/; also see "Why J&K Youth Are Opting For Guns," *The Milli Gazette*, April 28, 2015.

5. "Burhan Muzaffar Wani is the Bhagat Singh of Occupied Kashmir," *The Nation*, December 11, 2015.

6. Shah.

7. Shah.

8. Ibid.

9. "Burhan Muzaffar Wani is the Bhagat Singh of Occupied Kashmir," *The Nation*, December 11, 2015

10. Rohan Dua, "At 10, Burhan Wani wanted to join Indian Army: Father," *The Economic Times,* September 26, 2016; also see 'If my son was killed in encounter why his body didn't bear a bullet wound?' *The Indian Express*, April 14, 2015, accessed at: https://indianexpress.com/article/india/india-others/if-my-son-was-killed-in-encounter-why-his-body-didnt-bear-a-bullet-wound/

11. "Report on the Situation of Human Rights in Kashmir," Office of the United Nations High Commissioner for Human Rights, June 14, 2018, accessed at: https://reliefweb.int/report/india/report-situation-human-rights-kashmir-developments-indian-state-jammu-and-kashmir-june

12. UN Report, 2018.

13. Ibid.

14. Rifat Fareed, "At ground zero of Kashmir unrest, residents see no end to deaths," *Al Jazeera,* February 21, 2009, accessed at: https://www.aljazeera.com/news/2019/02/ground-kashmir-unrest-residents-deaths-190221113249615.html

15. Fareed.

16. Ibid.

17. Ibid.

18. Arik Hussain Malik, "What Drives Kashmir's Youth To Join Militancy," Review paper, *International Journal of Political Science*, 4(6): 231-235, July 4, 2016.

19. Haley Duschinski, Mona Bhan, Ather Zia and Cynthia Mahmood, eds., *Resisting Occupation in Kashmir: The Ethnography of Political Violence*, (University of Pennsylvania Press, U.S.: 2018), p.31.

20. Ibid, pp. 30-33.

21. Ibid.

9. Guardian

1. A reputed Kashmiri journalist, who wished to be anonymous, directed me to a young journalist named Zahid, who introduced me to Mughli. The original story, titled "The pain of a lonely mother," published in *Express India* in January 2009.

2. Details of mass graves are recorded in a preliminary report, *Buried Evidence*, published by the International People's Tribunal on Human Rights and Justice in Indian-administered Kashmir (December 2009).

3. This number has been cited by the Association of Parents of Disappeared Persons (APDP) based in Indian-held Kashmir, Human Rights Watch, The International People's Tribunal on Human Rights and Justice in Indian-administered Kashmir, and countless activists and journalists I've met in the valley accept this number.

10. Prisoners

1. Parashar, Swati, "Gender, Jihad and *Jingoism*," in *Studies in Conflict & Terrorism*, March 15, 2011, p. 304

2. Ibid, p.303

3. Human Rights Watch Report, January 2012, p. 2

4. "Hard to win hearts and minds in Kashmir," by Soumitro Das in *The Statesman*, October 19, 2013

5. Haroon Mirani, "Kashmir women police streets Taliban-style," in Women's eNews

6. BBC news report, "Taking the jihad to Kashmir's women," by Geeta Pandey, May 30, 2006, http://news.bbc.co.uk/2/hi/south_asia/5028844.stm

7. Email correspondence with Dr. Arif Maghribi in 2013; he also sent reports me that outlined his work with rape victims and their families

8. Asia Watch and Physicians for Human Rights, "Rape in Kashmir: A Crime of War," Vol. 5, Issue 9,

9. An article in *Kashmir Times* lists 5125 rape cases registered in Jammu and Kashmir since 1989, http://www.kashmirtimes.com/newsdet.aspx?q=23748

10. In November 2011, Sami jan met Asiya in her home and conducted an interview on my behalf.

Conclusion

1. Dexter Filkins, "Blood and Soil in Narendra Modi's India," December 9, 2019 issue.

2. Arundhati Roy, "Silence Is the Loudest Sound," *New York Times*, August 15, 2019. Accessed at: https://www.nytimes.com/2019/08/15/opinion/sunday/kashmir-siege-modi.html

3. Rifat Fareed, "Cut-off Kashmir resorts to primitive communication methods," DW, August 12, 2019. Accessed at https://www.dw.com/en/cut-off-kashmir-resorts-to-primitive-communication-methods/a-49993089

4. "Electric shocks, beatings: Kashmiris allege abuse by Indian army," *Al Jazeera*, September 10, 2019.

5. Hanifa, Aziz, "Rep. Pramila Jayapal's resolution on Kashmir, garners some traction, and angry Indian diaspora reaction," *India Abroad,* December 16, 2019. Accessed at: https://www.indiaabroad.com/india/rep-pramila-jayapals-resolution-on-kashmir-garners-some-traction-and-angry-indian-diaspora-reactions/article_f01508f0-207c-11ea-bbb0-4364052c8e64.html.

6. Ibid.

7. Wani, Riyaz, "India's new domicile law for Jammu & Kashmir is making residents anxious," *Quartz India*, April 7, 2020. Accessed at: https://qz.com/india/1834012/after-article-370-new-jammu-kashmir-domicile-law-fuels-anxiety/. Also see the statement issued by the Organization of Islamic Cooperation (OIC) on the Domicile Law, May 20, 2020. Accessed at: https://www.oic-oci.org/topic/?t_id=23430&t_ref=14015&lan=en; and "Central government defines domicile for J&K; those who have lived in UT for 15 years, registered migrants & students," *The Economic Times*, April 1, 2020, accessed at: https://economictimes.indiatimes.com/news/politics-and-nation/central-govt-defines-domicile-for-jk-those-who-have-lived-in-ut-for-15-yrs-registered-migrants-students/articleshow/74923952.cms

8. Wani, Riyaz, "India's new domicile law for Jammu & Kashmir is making residents anxious," *Quartz India*, April 7, 2020. Accessed at: https://qz.com/india/1834012/after-article-370-new-jammu-kashmir-domicile-law-fuels-anxiety/

From an award-winning speaker and scholar on conflicts. Farhana Qazi presents a heart-warming story of the people of Kashmir: their struggle, sacrifice, and the will to survive against all odds. In a land of militants and a majestic Army, women endure the brutalities of war. In this incredible journey, Qazi examines conflict from both sides of the border, moving across mountains in India and Pakistan to discover an unforgettable people.

Farhana Qazi is an American scholar and an internationally recognized speaker on conflicts in the Muslim world. She is the recipient of the 21st Century Leader Award from the National Committee on American Foreign Policy. She has appeared on CNN, BBC, MSNBC, PBS, and international news. To learn more, visit www.farhanaqazi.com.

NEWPORT PUBLISHING
Cover Design by
Farhana Qazi

Printed in Great Britain
by Amazon

72157735R00111